EDINBURGH CASTLE.

THE STONES OF SCOTLAND

1 EDINBURGH CASTLE FROM GREYFRIARS CHURCHYARD

From a Painting by
Robert Sivell, A.R.S.A.

THE STONES
OF SCOTLAND

Edited by

GEORGE SCOTT-MONCRIEFF

With Contributions by

W. Douglas Simpson, G. P. H. Watson,
W. Mackay Mackenzie, Ian G. Lindsay
and Ian C. Hannah

Illustrated from Photographs

LONDON
B. T. BATSFORD LTD.
15 NORTH AUDLEY STREET, W.1

First Published, June 1938

MADE AND PRINTED IN GREAT BRITAIN
FOR THE PUBLISHERS, B. T. BATSFORD LTD., LONDON
BY T. AND A. CONSTABLE LTD., EDINBURGH

CONTENTS

v

ACKNOWLEDGMENT

THE Publishers must acknowledge their obligation to the photographers whose work is reproduced in these pages, and whose names are given in the List of Illustrations. They are also indebted to Miss Norah Davenport for drawing the plans in the chapter on "The Church in Mediaeval Scotland," and to Dr. W. Mackay Mackenzie for the plans in the chapter on "Castles and Towers." The endpapers have been reproduced from Slezer's *Theatrum Scotiae*.

LIST OF ILLUSTRATIONS

2 Steeple of St. Giles' Church, Edinburgh

3 Culross Tolbooth, Fife

George Scott-Moncrieff

~~~~~~

INTRODUCTION

~~~~~~

THE sentimentality that encumbers Scottish History has done very little to give us any sensible pride in tradition. The result of this lack may be seen throughout the greater part of our country, where towers, town and country houses, and cottages stand in dismal disrepair and imminent decay. Those who should be responsible custodians, who own, or have owned, the gems of Scottish architecture, have too often shifted their allegiances elsewhere: or have become too poor and have neglected the homes of their forebears, or too rich and made a mess of them. The generality of people, who might under happier circumstances protest against much of this destruction of that most patent side of their country's heritage, its history and taste in stone, seem not to associate white-harled stonework, crowsteps and corbelled stair-towers with intrinsic aesthetic or historic values. They are confused with ideas of half-timbering, and also, no doubt, Scots have too long turned their eyes unto the hills to the neglect of the smaller beauties of their landskip.

Half-timbering is, of course, foreign to Scotland (or was, until the coming of the roadhouse), and practically no sizable building erected in Scotland before 1700 has the dominating characteristics of English work. What then does the Scottish tradition in architecture signify? The five writers who contribute the text of this book analyse

the various developments that took place. Dr. Simpson as an archaeo-
logist considers the early stones, the dwelling-places, and monuments
of our forebears in prehistoric times and in the early days of history.
At once there are fundamental distinctions between the works on
either side of the Border. Mr. Watson traces the development of
ecclesiastical architecture up to the Reformation. The Scots showed
a liking for the Romanesque that entailed its retention, with local
characteristics, long after England was developing her peculiar
forms of Gothic: what Gothic we have is not even predominantly
English in inspiration but derives more directly from the French.
In his chapter on castles and towers Dr. Mackay Mackenzie explains
the functions of the castle, and how there also shapes and forms
grew as it were out of the landskip and the problems it presented,
until, when the original functions ceased to have great importance,
these forms were developed as decoration and as insignia of the
nobleman's prosperity. Mr. Lindsay indicates how these same
forms were translated for the later dwellings in the burghs, and,
in what is perhaps the first analysis of its kind, defines the nature
and development of the Scottish burgh. He deals with such
characteristics of the Scottish scene as the tolbooth, the mercat
cross and the doocot. His remarks and those of Mr. Hannah on
the post-Reformation churches are particularly apposite, for there
are good churches built by the Presbyterians, although they seem
to be the last to realise it and today would wish to embellish with
mock-Gothic windows churches that have been built for the
functions originally demanded by a Puritan religion. To spoil the
proportions of such churches by installing structural anachronisms
is to maintain the baleful traditions of those Reformers who have
already done us such ubiquitous harm in those direct efforts to divorce
beauty from faith that culminated only in ornamentation without
beauty. Professor Hannah takes the history from the time of Sir
William Bruce and the Adam family into the first years of the last
century, when the New Town of Edinburgh closed, at least for the
time, the creditable side of the story with an outburst of formal
splendour.

But the written word of itself is inadequate to convey an architectural tradition; analysis and history are rather the aids to a
maturer understanding, the bridges that connect with other com-

partments of our awareness. Here then are photographs that more
directly present the qualities of Scottish masonry. In our choice of
photographs we have tried as far as is practicable to eliminate the
eternal ruin—too much of our heritage is in that state—concen-
trating rather upon what is still with us. I for one cannot truly
enjoy a visit to Dryburgh Abbey, or Melrose Abbey, or even
Sweetheart Abbey. At St. Andrews the toothless remnants of the
Cathedral depress me immoderately. Apart from their interest
ruins have, no doubt, their own charm, sung too often by the
romantics of the last century, but a living building has a far greater
relevance. What was intended by those who conceived it remains,
not translated into terms of wreckage but still vital : not depending
upon association but upon form.

It is with quite different feelings that I remember a first sight of
the Argyll Lodging in Stirling; three sides of a square with tall
pointed towers in the corners and rich mouldings on door and lintel.
Then Traquair, that indescribable barrier of stone, pierced by small
windows, its solemnity just broken by three turrets, the whole
magnificently a piece with the surrounding trees and the great
closed gates. More massive yet is that double-barrelled tower of
hewn stone, Borthwick Castle, on its steep mound at the head of a
watercourse. In the sunlight it is a soft yellow split by a black
sunless shadow, the machicolations beneath its parapet meticulously
picked out in light and shade, its superstructure silhouetted against
the sky. In Aberdeen a common lodging-house threatened with
demolition, 'Cumberland' House, still stands while the well-
affected fight for its preservation, a broken scrap of street but
even in disrepair with interest and quality lacking in the neighbouring buildings. Within, coloured packmen sit round the fireplace in a room of broken panelling, and beds stand in rows beneath
fine plaster ceilings.

Happy again is Culross Palace, now restored, the property of
the National Trust for Scotland: its shapely dormered buildings
stand by the shore in front of a terraced garden. Craigievar
is order out of chaos; there seems to be no plan to it, yet on every
side it is satisfying, showing fresh aspects. The late Mansfield
Forbes said of it that it was like a book, as one walked round it
it seemed to open and close, now narrow, now stretching wide; in

line and detail it is dynamic. Very different is the state of Aldie
Castle, perfectly situated on the edge of the Cleish Hills; it was
built at three periods of the sixteenth century, the original handsome tower developed round the smallest of courtyards with a
watchful window looking down on the entry: well within living
memory it was intact, and even now could be turned into the
most delightful modern home. 'The buildings at present are
falling into a state of ruin the more regrettable since, if the roofs
were made good, a most interesting laird's house could be
preserved,' says the Inventory of the Office of Works.

One is continually surprised by these towers and their descendant
forms; compact buildings with stair-towers gracefully corbelled
out, they achieve an appearance often of great size where they are
in fact small, well meriting present-day habitation.

Amisfield Tower in Dumfriesshire conveys the sense of the
Scottish tower to a nicety: the bare lower walls flower into a
flourish of corbelling, turret, and bartisan, the hard lines become
fluid, the contrast complete. Unfortunately detailed study of the
transition from the tower to the mansion—well represented by
Pilmuir in East Lothian—has fallen outside the scope of any of the
chapters. Auchendinny House is an early example of the mansion
in Scotland, to which Airds and Arniston are the successors.
It stands behind outrunners, low buildings on either side that
enhance the whole with an agreeable sense of mass. I have seen
a manse of this type, beautifully placed above the red bay of Apple-
cross, deserted. Stirling Palace is not deserted but used as barracks
—a dubious consolation; as Sir John Stirling Maxwell has said, its
condition is a disgrace to us. St. Andrews, as its citizens are
beginning to realise, is more remarkable for the seventeenth and
eighteenth century houses that still stand in its wide streets than
for the moither of stone that was once a cathedral.

In a book of this length it has of course been impossible to
cover every aspect of Scottish building. Much of the lesser detail
has had to be passed over with, at best, inadequate comment—as,
for example, the painted ceilings, one of the most pleasing refine-
ments of the pre-eighteenth-century Scottish interior, of which a
number have lately been discovered well preserved beneath later
plaster. Vaulting, common in the lower apartments, gracefully

4 Cemetery Chapel, Arbroath (late Presbyterian)

5 Dunnet Church, Caithness (early Presbyterian)

6 The Argyll Lodging, Stirling

7 Deans' Court, through Pend, St. Andrews

8 Wade's Bridge over the Tay at Aberfeldy

9 The Bridge at Dunans, Glendaruel, Argyll

10 Wade's Bridge of Orchy, Argyll, constructed about 1750

gives a sense of solidity in stone, carried on by newel stairs and window-seats howked out of thick walls. Scottish ironwork has a massy quality. Rooms of good proportion frame in their windows views of the landskip to which these houses are native. A whole chapter might have been written about the old bridges over our watercourses whose beauty of line merits their retention even where their function must devolve upon a modern fabric.

Enlightened appreciation of the past may result in the creditable side to the story being taken up again today, after an age in which the fancies of untrammelled romantics perpetrated every kind of folly, and most kinds of monstrosities—witness the baronial halls of business barons, the nineteenth-century parish churches, tolbooths and mausoleums, the villas with applied turrets that mock those that seem to grow out of the old buildings. Sir Robert Lorimer, although the quality of his work is by no means constant, had a genuine sense of the values that inspired the native traditions. More important to today, Charles Rennie Mackintosh, who to our shame worked too little in Scotland, was essentially indebted to the vital, and never fully consummated, tradition of pre-1700 Scottish architecture. But it is forty years since the Glasgow School of Art was built, in Scotland Mackintosh has been neglected, and we have an unceasing stream of shoddy, denationalised and uninspired building. It is not that there are no good architects—they may be few but they do exist; and the pathetic paralysis of our industry that makes it cheaper to import unsuitable building materials than to work our own quarries is only a contributory cause: the main blame lies with the indifference of the Scottish people. I hope that the five essays in this book may help towards a more general sensibility in respect both of the past and of what is to come.

W. Douglas Simpson
D.Lit.

◇◇

THE

EARLY STONES

◇◇

THE earliest dwelling-places of mankind about which we know anything in Scotland are certain caves, such as those of Druim-vargie near Oban and Inchnadamph in Sutherland, and the camping sites, now traceable by their refuse dumps, found on the 25-foot raised beach around our coasts. The tools of flint, bone, and deer-horn recovered from such sites seem to indicate that their makers lived in what is known as the Azilian period, at the close of Palaeo-lithic or Old Stone Age times. Probably this was at least 10,000 years ago. These Azilian folk seem to have been a wandering people in a low state of culture, ignorant of husbandry and settled life, who eked out a precarious existence by hunting and fishing. It is likely that they were degenerated descendants of the Palaeolithic hunters of the Continent and South Britain, who followed the rein-deer into Scotland as the climate of the Ice Age tempered and glacial conditions retreated northward. In recent years discoveries have been made, in various parts of Scotland, of the characteristic micro-lithic or 'pigmy' flint implements which are generally supposed to belong to the Tardenoisian period, that succeeded the Azilian and marks the transition from Palaeolithic to Neolithic or New Stone Age times. Some of these tools reveal considerable technical skill in their fashioning; but of constructional ability the peoples of this early time appear to have had little or none. At least, neither

6

house nor tomb belonging to Azilian or Tardenoisian times has yet been discovered.

The next race to inhabit Scotland had developed considerable civilisation. They had abandoned the wandering existence of the Palaeolithic people for a settled agricultural or pastoral life, and had tamed the dog, horse, ox, sheep, goat, and pig. They had invented the arts of polishing stone, of weaving, and of making pottery, which they fashioned in exceedingly tasteful and well-made forms. Above all, they had learned to commemorate their noble dead by heaping together huge cairns containing chambers in which the bodies were laid; and it is with these chambered cairns of the Neolithic period that the history of construction in Scotland begins. They are typically oval or elongated in shape, and in the extreme north of Scotland they are often found with curious projections, or horns, at the corners. Some of these cairns are of enormous size, attaining a length of as much as 240 feet. They show very clearly that the people of this early period must have possessed considerable powers of combined effort and no mean constructional skill. The burial chamber is usually at one end of the cairn, and is subdivided by partition walls: it would seem that such cairns served as family vaults through several generations. The dead were either cremated or inhumed, and from their skeletons it is possible to infer the physical characteristics and racial affinities of the Neolithic population. They were of medium height, slightly built, with a peculiar long-shaped head and oval face. Anthropologists believe that this race belonged to the great dark-featured, Mediterranean group of peoples, of whom the Basques are today a remnant. This man of the Neolithic period seems to have entered Scotland by the west from Ireland, and to have slowly overspread the west and north of the country. Of the abodes which he constructed for his dead, we now know a good deal; of his living abodes, none have survived, unless we may count as such three pit-dwellings found at Glenluce, which seem to belong to this period.

The finest chambered tomb that the Neolithic Age has left to us in Britain is Maeshowe, on Main Island, Orkney. This vast sepulchre, 92 feet in diameter and 30 feet in height, is an earthen mound, not a cairn, though its central core is stony and encloses a beautifully built rectangular chamber, probably

20 feet in height, with internal buttresses at the corners and three cells opening one on each side, except where the passage, 54 feet in length, enters the chamber. Round the mound is a mighty ditch, nearly 40 feet in width. Unfortunately no relics have been found in Maeshowe, for it was pillaged by Viking robbers in or before the twelfth century. These tomb-breakers have left their runic inscriptions on its walls, from which we learn that some of them had been *Jorsalafarar*, *i.e.* pilgrims to Jerusalem.

Towards the end of the Stone Age—perhaps about 2000 B.C.— there appeared in Scotland the pioneers of the round-headed races who ultimately introduced the use of bronze. These new-comers generally inhumed their dead singly in 'short cists' of stone slabs neatly fitted together. Numerous examples have been found all over the eastern parts of the country. The skeletons recovered from them reveal a people of moderate stature and powerful physique, with round, straight-backed heads, and square, determined jaws. The body is always buried in a crouched position; and among the grave goods is usually an urn, supposed to have contained food for the journey to the next world. Small quantities of charcoal are often found in these short cist graves. So far as our present knowledge goes, this people would appear to have entered Scotland along the eastern Lowlands, and their pottery has been traced back to Holland and the Rhine basin. Landing probably in more than one place on the British coast, they spread gradually to the west and north, and reached Arran in the one direction and Shetland and the Hebrides in the other, at a time when in all these localities their Neolithic predecessors were still burying their dead in the chambered cairns: indeed, there is distinct evidence that the new-comers peacefully penetrated among the older population and intermingled with them.

After the introduction of bronze, which took place probably about 1800 B.C., came in the practice of cremation, the ashes of the dead being enclosed in large cinerary urns. This fashion of burning the bodies began in South Britain during the short cist period. It spread very rapidly, and is found in late Neolithic burials in northern Scotland—in which district, among others, cremation and inhumation appear to have been practised simultaneously throughout the chambered cairn period. The burial cairns of the

11 Standing-Stones of Stenness, Orkney

12 Standing-Stones at Callanish, Lewis

13 Dun Dornadilla, Glen More, Sutherland

Bronze Age are typically round in shape, and some of them are of great size, as much as 90 feet in diameter. As a rule, the cairns both of the Stone and Bronze Ages tend to occupy commanding sites, ranging up to as much as 1000 feet above sea-level.

The Bronze Age folk seem also to have been the architects of the stone circles in which Scotland is so prolific, as these, when excavated, have often yielded cinerary urns and grave goods of this period. It is now believed that the Scottish stone circles are derived from the peristalith or ring of boulders which is usually found placed round the margin of a Neolithic chambered cairn. Many different types of stone circle have been noted. In particular, in the north-eastern knuckle of Scotland—beyond a line drawn from Bervie to Spey Bay, but mostly between Dee and Deveron—there is a remarkable group of stone circles, characterised by the presence, on the southern (generally the south-western) segment of the circle, of a large horizontal or recumbent stone, set between two of the pillars. More than seventy circles of this special type have been noted, and many others have doubtless disappeared. Fantastic ideas have been prevalent about the meaning and use of these circles of standing stones. In particular they have been widely regarded as 'Druidical,' although excavation has shown that they date from long before the Druids, and there is otherwise no evidence that Druids had anything to do with them. Recent exploration of some of the Aberdeenshire circles, of the recumbent stone type, has shown that they continued to be used as burial grounds until the Hallstatt period, or earlier part of the Iron Age.

One of the most interesting groups of prehistoric monuments in Scotland is the series of three round cairns at Clava, near Nairn, which are surrounded by rings of standing stones. Two of the cairns are genuine examples of the Neolithic chambered type, with a passage of access, but the third has no passage, and its central chamber does not seem to have been roofed. The whole group, therefore, strikingly illustrates the degeneration of the chambered cairn into the ring cairn with central burial stance, and at the same time the evolution of the true stone circle from the ring of stones bordering the cairn. Of the stone circles, much the most striking example in Scotland is the one at Callanish, on the west side of Lewis. It has been truly described as 'ranking second in import-

ance to Stonehenge among the Bronze Age monuments of Britain.'
Here we have a circle of thirteen pillar stones, standing at the end
of an avenue of pillars, 270 feet in length, while from the circle
extend, like the head and arms of a cross, three single rows of
stones.   In addition to all this, there is a chambered cairn within
the circle.

Probably to the Bronze Age belong the remarkable rows of
standing stones, sometimes arranged fanwise so as to converge
upon a round cairn, which are found in certain parts of Scotland,
notably in Caithness.   They remind one of the famous multiple
settings of standing stones at Carnac in Brittany.

On many of our stone circles and solitary standing stones, as
well as on natural boulders and live rock surfaces, cup-marks are
found.   In some cases these cup-marks are ringed, as many as eight
rings having been found around a single cup; while occasionally
a runnel or gutter extends from the cup across the rings.   Nothing
is known as to the purpose of such mysterious sculpturings.   Their
distribution, and other considerations, suggest that they were introduced via the west coast, from Ireland and, more remotely, from
Spain, where the closest parallels to our cup-mark patterns are
found.

It is in the Bronze Age that we begin to meet with clear evidence
of the domestic habitations of the people.   In many parts of Scotland groups of small round cairns, often less than 15 feet in diameter,
are found, which seem to be of the Bronze Age and probably represent the burial places of the rank and file of the people: and close
beside these are hut circles, which can hardly be other than the
remains of the habitations of the communities that buried their
dead in the adjacent cairns.

About the year 400 B.C. the use of iron was introduced into
Scotland.   At this time, the inhabitants of Scotland were, comparatively speaking, a highly civilised race, skilled in various arts
and crafts, and distinguished particularly by their constructive
genius.   That genius, no less than their power of combined effort
and capacity for organisation, is revealed in the immense stone
hill forts, sometimes vitrified, and the crannogs or pile dwellings
which they built as refuges in time of war, and on a smaller scale,
in the earth houses which they constructed as subterranean adjuncts

14 Broch at Mousa, Shetland

15 Broch at Glenelg, Inverness-shire

16 Skara Brae, Orkney

17 Jarlshof, Shetland

PREHISTORIC STONE DWELLINGS

to their hut-dwellings. In particular must we admire their skill in conceiving and building those unique and fascinating structures, the brochs, concerning which the late Dr. Joseph Anderson, than whom none certainly was better qualified to judge, remarked that 'the concentration of effort towards the two main objects of space for shelter and complete security was never more strikingly exhibited, and no more admirable adaptation of materials so simple and common as undressed and uncemented stone has ever been discovered or suggested.'

Such impressive structures as our Scottish hill forts represent something more significant than the mere proof, striking though that proof may be, of the technical skill and resource of their ancient builders. They speak to us across the ages about the growth of those political conditions which have created the Scottish nation. The conditions that drove the early tribes to erect these massive and enduring structures for their refuge must have been conditions of constant stress. Larger political units were forming and tribal warfare was assuming a grander scale.

Three main types of these hill forts may be recognised. In one, exemplified by the Brown Caterthun in Angus and the fort on Barra Hill in Aberdeenshire, the ramparts are of earthwork. In the second class, they are massively built of dry-stone walling, sometimes as much as 20 or 25 feet in thickness. Three examples of this second class—Forgandenny and Abernethy in Strathtay, and Burghead on the Moray Firth—have a bonding structure of beams, traversing the wall from back to front. This type of construction was noted by Julius Caesar in certain of the hill-top towns that he besieged in Gaul. The third class are known as vitrified forts, because in them the stones have been partially fused together by the application of intense heat. About sixty of these have been recorded in Scotland. The best known are Dunagoil in Bute, Finavon in Angus, Tap o' Noth and Dunnideer in Aberdeenshire, and Knock Farrel in Ross-shire.

Very little excavation has been done upon our Scottish hill forts; but so far as the results go, they indicate that the period of occupation of these forts was more or less coincident with the Roman invasions. It may be noted that one fort, on Bennachie in Aberdeenshire, has a well-defined parapet and 'fire-step.' This feature is found in certain Welsh tribal forts known to have been erected during the Roman occupation, and with the sanction of the imperial authorities; and it is probably due to Roman engineering influence.

Some of our larger Scottish hill forts were permanently occupied, and are in reality hill-top towns, such as Caesar found among the Gauls. Of these the best known example is Traprain Law in East Lothian, which has yielded a rich harvest of relics showing a continuous occupation during the first four centuries A.D., as well as the famous silver hoard, the 'Treasure of Traprain,' representing the loot of Roman villas and Christian churches, buried on the hill probably soon after the year 400.

But the most remarkable prehistoric fortifications in Scotland are the brochs, and of these she may well be proud, for nothing like them is known anywhere else in the world. They are circular towers of dry-built masonry, with walls 12 or 15 feet in thickness, and probably 40 or 50 feet in height, enclosing an open court, usually about 30 or 35 feet in diameter. The thick walls are hollowed into galleries, reached by a stair which winds round the tower to the parapet. Round the inside there was, in most cases, a kind of penthouse, supported on posts. Many brochs have outbuildings clustered around them, usually within a defensible rampart. Relics dug out of the brochs prove them to belong to the latest phase of the prehistoric Iron Age: Roman pottery and knick-knacks, which must have found their way into them by trade, are of common occurrence in broch excavations. It is clear that they were not merely places of refuge but were continuously occupied by chiefs dwelling among their retainers, very much like the feudal system and its castles in the Middle Ages. The brochs are mainly found in the north and west of Scotland, where they seem to have been evolved from the small *duns* or forts, sometimes galleried, which are so common in the Hebrides. Beyond the main broch area there are some notable outliers—for example, the Tappuck broch in the Torwood, Stirlingshire, and the broch of Cockburn Law in the Whitadder valley, Berwickshire. The finest remaining broch is on the island of Mousa, in the Shetlands. It still survives to a height of 45 feet.

To the same period as the brochs belong the crannogs or lake-dwellings, artificial islands of mingled earth and stone, strongly framed together with timber and pegged down by piles; and also the earth-houses, subterranean galleries, often as much as 80 or 90 feet in length, with dry-stone side walls corbelled inwards above, so as to support large stone roofing-slabs. These earth-houses seem, in many cases, to have been adjuncts to huts above-ground. They were assuredly not places of refuge, since the hut would betray their presence to an enemy. Nor were they mere stores, for they were certainly lived in: midden deposits and hearths are found in them, and some have even chimneys. Probably the inhabitants sought shelter in them from the cold of winter. Tacitus, in his description of Germany, tells how some of the inhabitants there were accustomed to dig caves in the earth, into which they retired in winter. Many of the tribes whom Tacitus listed as *Germani* are known to have been of Celtic stock, and it is probable that the underground dwellings of which he had heard were earth-houses similar to those constructed by their Caledonian kinsmen. Two Scottish earth-houses have been partly built out of stones taken from Roman camps in the vicinity.

In the Hebrides, and in the northern isles, where the rigours of winter are excessively severe, the ordinary hut circle, whose superstructure was of wattle, loaded with clay, gives place to the wheel dwelling, a circular edifice, enclosing a central court, and divided by radial walls into a series of chambers, not unlike the cross-section of an orange.

No account of the dwellings of the prehistoric Iron Age in Scotland would be complete without some mention of Skara Brae, the famous 'Pictish village' in Orkney. This is a collection of eight huts, built of untooled stones and roofed over, it would seem, with turf or skins, all the huts being linked together by narrow roofed galleries, and the whole establishment being blanketed in its own midden refuse, heaped round the walls for purposes of shelter against wind and driving sand. The inhabitants were a very primitive community, living on their flocks and herds, and on the shell-fish which they gathered from the beach beside their village. Although no metal tools or traces of metal were recorded during the excavations, the general *facies* of the constructions seems to belong to the Iron Age; some at least of the relics were of Iron

Age affinities, and metal tools undoubtedly were used in making certain of the objects. A somewhat higher state of civilisation is revealed by a similar settlement, more recently exposed, at Jarlshof in Shetland.

The repeated invasions of Scotland by the Roman armies, and their partial occupation of the country as far north as Strathmore, have left important monumental traces, in the marching camps which extend up into Aberdeenshire, in permanent military stations like Birrens in Dumfriesshire or Inchtuthil beyond the Tay, and in the Antonine Wall with its chain of forts betwixt Forth and Clyde. But impressive though these structures are, and great as has been the attention paid to them by modern Scottish antiquaries, strictly speaking they form no part of the monumental history of Scotland, for they represent an intrusive civilisation that failed to take root in our country—a mere episode which did not permanently or greatly affect her national development.

But where Rome had failed with the sword she returned to conquer by the Cross; and the earliest current of Christianity that flowed into what is now Scotland was a direct offshoot from the Roman occupation of Britain. This is clearly shown in the oldest Christian monuments that have been found in the country, namely, the inscribed and cross-marked stones of Whithorn and Kirkmadrine in Galloway—that is, in the district immediately affected by St. Ninian's mission and the foundation of his *Candida Casa* at Whithorn in 397. These stones bear inscriptions in the debased Latin language and script of the Lower Empire; they exhibit the Chi-Rho symbol (or sacred monogram of Christ's name), the Alpha and Omega, and the *Hic iacet* formula, all commonly found on Christian tombs throughout the Western Empire: and they commemorate persons with Latin or Latinised Celtic names.

In early Christian times Scotland was divided into four kingdoms, those of the Picts, the Scots, the Britons, and the Angles. For a long time the dominant member in this unruly partnership was the Kingdom of the Picts. In not a few respects the Picts were a remarkable people, and their civilisation was both vigorous in quality and highly individual in character. This is chiefly seen in the unique development of symbolic art which marked the sculptured monuments of Pictland during the early Christian period—

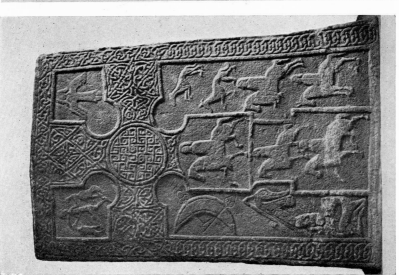

18 Cross-Slab, Rossie Priory,
Perthshire

(Back)

(Front)

19, 20 Cross-Slab, Invergowrie, Perthshire

STONE SLABS

23 Bressay Stone, Shetland

22 Cross-Slab, 'St. Orland's Stone,' at Cossins, Angus

21 Cross-Slab at Glamis, Angus

say between the fifth and the tenth centuries. Under a set of influences and with an evolutionary origin alike entirely unknown to us, there was developed among the Picts of the north-east, during those centuries, a highly elaborated, rigidly conventional, and at the same time extremely artistic code of symbolism, to the hidden meaning of which no solution, nay, not even the vestige of a solution, has been discovered. Nothing even faintly resembling it is known anywhere else in the world. This symbolism is marked by two very significant characteristics. In the first place, save for one or two stray 'outliers,' it is entirely confined to the districts known to have been inhabited by the Picts; and within these limits it is distinctively and overwhelmingly a product of the north-eastern Lowlands. In the second place, the forms of the symbols wherever they are found, from the Shetlands to Galloway, and from Aberdeen-shire to the Outer Isles, are so uniform and so highly conventionalised that it is clear we stand in the presence of a fully articulated, well-understood, and widespread system of ideographic art, the development of which must be accounted an astonishing manifestation of the Pictish genius.

Comparative study of these monuments shows that they fall into three classes, and it has been found possible approximately to delimit the chronological horizon of each class:

Class I (before A.D. 800).—Unshapen and undressed monoliths with incised symbols only. Of these, well-nigh half the total number recorded come from the district between the Dee and the Spey.

Class II (about A.D. 800-1000).—Slabs roughly tooled and shaped, having in addition to the symbols a cross of Celtic pattern, and often elaborate figure and animal groups, derived from the Bestiaries or from Early Christian symbolism; the sculpture now being in relief, and the symbols and cross alike enriched with more or less complex ornamentation in the School of Celtic art.

Class III (from about A.D. 1000 to the extinction of native Celtic art by the Anglo-Norman infiltration in the twelfth and thirteenth centuries).—Slabs on which the symbols have now disappeared, so that there remains only the Celtic cross, carved in relief and often sumptuously decorated.

An interesting fact is that the stones of Class II are very much less numerous than those either of Class I or Class III. This suggests that the transitional period was a short one compared with the first and the third periods—*i.e.* that once the cross came into use the symbolism died out fairly rapidly. It is also clear that during the second period the lead in production passed out of granitic and schistose Aberdeenshire into the sandstone districts flanking it, where the stone is more suitable for carving the richly decorated monuments of Classes II and III.

Whether the symbols were in their origin Pagan or Christian has been much disputed. All that can be said meantime is that their associations, where determinable, are always Christian. Stones both of Class I and of Class II occur again and again at known early Celtic church sites. Even where the primitive symbol stone stands now unassociated with any ascertained religious site, we must remember that all knowledge of an early wattled or timber church may long since have perished. On the other hand, it can of course be argued that it was the practice of the early missionaries to plant their churches at heathen sacred places, where such symbol stones, if the symbolism began by being pre-Christian, may well have stood. There is, in fact, evidence that the early chapels were frequently planted at or near the stone circles of the old Pagan faiths. This was more or less in accordance with the advice given by Gregory the Great to St. Augustine, the first missionary to the English, not to destroy the heathen temples but to convert them into churches, 'so that the people may, forsaking their error, be moved oft to haunt their wonted places to the honour and service of God.' So also there is a record of St. Patrick dedicating to Christ three heathen pillar stones. One case occurs in Aberdeenshire where symbols are incised on one of a group of two standing stones assignable presumably to the Bronze Age: but here the symbols may be secondary. It is at all events clear that the symbolism was capable in its entirety of having a Christian meaning, as is shown by its association with the cross on the monuments of Class II. The symbols have also been found inscribed on objects of metal and bone, and rudely carved on natural rock surfaces.

Equally mysterious is the sudden way in which this symbolism seems to blossom forth, as it were like Pallas from the head of Zeus, as a fully developed and highly elaborated art. Even on the

25 Cross, Kilmartin, Argyll

24 St. Martin's Cross, Iona (East side)

CROSSES

28 Detail
Mackinnon's Cross, Iona

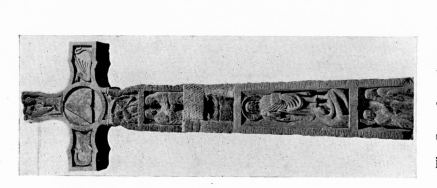

27 The Cross from the South
THE RUTHWELL CROSS

26 Detail on the East Side

oldest stones the symbols appear as a mature, extremely conventionalised, systematic, and determinate corpus of ideographic art,
which must surely have had a long evolutionary history behind it.
But of its more primitive development no trace appears to exist.
It has sometimes been suggested that the rude representations of
the symbols cut or scratched on the walls of certain caves may
represent such an earlier stage of development. But these are
plainly the amateur *graffiti* of hermits, whereas the symbols on the
monument are the work of skilled carvers trained in the special
conventions of their art. Such an argument would be about equal
to suggesting that a boy's name rudely cut on a tree-trunk must
necessarily be older than an inscription finely carved on a gravestone.

As to the meaning of the symbols, it is impossible even to guess.
Some have thought that the strange geometrical forms must be
fraught with a significance purely abstract or metaphysical. On
the other hand, some of them, such as the 'mirror' and the 'comb,'
are obviously real things, and the way in which the 'crescent' and
the 'double disc' symbols on many of the stones of Class II are
enriched with Celtic ornament almost irresistibly impels one to the
idea that they are portrayals of real objects in metal-work. Nay,
more, an actual example of the 'crescent and V-rod' combination
in metal has been found: but, as if on purpose to baffle us, on the
back of this is graven the 'double disc and Z-rod.' Others have
suggested that the symbols are badges or insignia of rank or office;
but a serious objection to this view is that they sometimes occur
in groups of two or three on one stone, or the same symbol may be
repeated three times on the same monument. Also, it is a trifle
difficult to conceive what the purpose might be of specifying rank
or office on a monument that is otherwise anonymous. It would be
like erecting a tombstone with the inscription 'In memory of a
Lieut.-Colonel' or 'Here lies a Clerk of the Peace'! Nor can they
be tribal badges, for no single one of the symbols is confined to
any particular territorial area of Pictland.

A very interesting point is raised by the manner in which the
symbols are combined. Thus, while both the 'crescent' and the
'double disc' are found by themselves, and also traversed by a
'rod,' the 'rod' is never found alone. It is therefore clear that the
'crescent' and the 'double disc' have a meaning by themselves, but

D

that the 'rod' has no independent meaning: it merely modifies, in some way, the meaning of the symbol with which it is associated. Moreover, the 'rod' which is applied to the 'crescent' is always the 'V-rod,' and that applied to the 'double disc' is always the 'Z-rod': the 'double disc' never has the 'V-rod,' nor the 'crescent' the 'Z-rod.' Similarly, the 'mirror' and 'comb,' where they are found along with other symbols, are always placed beneath them. It is clear, therefore, that the combinations always occur in a constant and never in a haphazard way.

Not only is this 'Pictish symbolism' confined to those parts of Scotland which the Picts are known to have inhabited, but within the old Scotic colony of Dalriada the typical cross-form is free-standing—like the two well-known crosses of St. John and St. Martin in Iona, or the Kildalton Cross in Islay—whereas east of the central mountain backbone the cross, in all save a few late cases, is graven on a slab. We find, therefore, that Scotland north of the Forth is divided into two monumental areas, corresponding, more or less, to the ancient kingdoms of Pictland and Dalriada. In Strathclyde and in Bernicia, again, the early Christian monuments have a character of their own. Inscriptions in the Ogham or old Celtic alphabet, and in Anglian or Norse runes, are associated with a number of our Scottish monuments: the Ogham inscriptions, however, do not occur in the country south of the Forth and Clyde.

The most famous of the early Christian monuments of Scotland is the Ruthwell Cross, which ranks among the foremost examples of Dark Age art in Europe. On it is inscribed, in Anglian runes, a celebrated poem in which, with a thoroughly Teutonic, and indeed largely Pagan, spirit the Cross itself describes its part and emotion in the greatest of sagas, the tragedy of Our Lord's Passion:

> Then the Young Hero, who was mightiest God,
>   Strong and with steadfast mind
> Up to the Cross with steps unfaltering trod,
>   There to redeem mankind.
> I trembled, but I durst not fail:
> I on my shoulders bare the Glorious King.
> They pierce my sides with many a darksome nail,
> And on us both their cruel curses fling.

Taken all together, the early Christian monuments of Scotland form a rich *corpus* of native art, all of which is full of vigour, while the best examples are of very high aesthetic merit indeed. When sculptured stones, so beautiful and so refined, are dug up in the homes of the ancient civilisations in Greece or Italy, Egypt or Mesopotamia, no end of a fuss is made about them: they are illustrated in our newspapers, and the public is taught to venerate them as the products of a classic civilisation, to which our own land is supposed to offer no parallel. Yet here in Scotland, unregarded by all save a few enthusiasts, are those abundant proofs of what Dr. Joseph Anderson most truly called 'a manifestation of artistic culture altogether unparalleled in Europe.' To the average Scotsman, even their existence is unknown. Casts of them are almost entirely lacking in our art galleries, which prefer to fill their sculpture courts with replicas of second-rate Roman copies of lost Greek originals, while ignoring the beautiful remains of our own native art—a heritage which a people rightly conscious of its past ought to hold in the highest regard.

The Celtic Church was organised on a coenobitic basis, and from stray hints scattered through Adamnan's biography of St. Columba we can obtain a fairly clear idea of what a Celtic monastery in the earliest period was like, with its group of wooden or wattled huts, each for a single brother, floored with beaten earth; its barn, stable, and byre; its mill, its bakery, its kiln for corn-drying; its refectory for the common meal, its guests' house, and its little heather-thatched church of logs, with a sacristy opening on one side, where the monastic bell was kept. Somewhat apart from the rest stood the Abbot's house, and the whole establishment was surrounded by a cashel, that is, a fencible dry-built wall or earthen bank. Afterwards, these wooden or wattled buildings came to be replaced in stone; and of Celtic monasteries belonging to this later type there are still some interesting remains in the remoter parts of the country. Probably the most complete is on *Eileach-an-Naoimh*, the Rock of the Saint, one of the Garvelloch Islands. The remains comprise two chapels, a double-chambered beehive hut, an underground cell, a kiln, a sculptured cross of late date, at least two graveyards, and a well, *Tobar Challuim-chille*, St. Columba's Spring. Part of the cashel is still preserved. In the Island of Skye are two very interesting monastic sites, Loch Chaluim-chille in Trotternish and Annait near Dunvegan. Loch Chaluim-chille is now drained, and the island on which stood the monastery forms a dry stony tump rising above meadows fragrant with natural hay. The remains are still very distinct, and give a good idea of a primitive Celtic monastery, with its enclosing cashel, its beehive cells, and its two small chapels. Annait is probably the earliest Christian settlement in Skye: the name means 'mother-church.' The site is a promontory between two deep basaltic gulleys; and the thick enclosing wall is well seen, with the foundations of a chapel and beehive cells. The Brough of Deerness, a tidal islet in Orkney, has the remains of another of these early monastic establishments. A small church, built with lime, stands amid a group of eighteen uncemented oval or subrectangular cells, all enclosed by a cashel.

Little or nothing is known about the dates of the primitive chapels which still exist in ruins on many of the Western Isles, but some of them at all events belong to very early types. For example, on North Rona there is a double-chambered church of exceedingly rude construction. The eastern chamber is older than the western, and evidently formed a tiny chapel, which became the chancel when the western chamber, forming a nave, was added. In the original part, which measures only 11 feet 6 inches by 7 feet, the side walls converge as they rise, after the Irish manner. At first the masonry was dry-built, but at a later date it has been pointed with lime. Nothing could be cruder or more primitive in aspect than this little church. Close beside it are some beehive dwellings, attached to a rectangular enclosure.

One solitary example of these primitive Celtic churches survives on the east coast, the little cell on Inchcolm which is thought to have been occupied by the hermit who in 1123 afforded shelter to King Alexander, 'constraint be violent tempest to remane three dayes' on the island. This modest structure measures about 16 feet by 6 feet internally, and is very irregularly shaped, but built with mortar. Whatever its original date, it has evidently been much repaired during the period of the Augustinian Priory, and the roof which is a true vault, of pointed section, is certainly not older than the thirteenth century.

Sloping jambs, in the Celtic or insular manner, are to be seen in the little chancelled church of Lybster, in the parish of Reay, in Caithness.

29 St. Clement's Church, Rodil, Harris

30 Dunglass Church, East Lothian

32   The Round Tower, Abernethy, Perthshire

31   The Round Tower at Brechin Cathedral, Angus

Scotland still retains two examples of the free-standing, tall, tapering round towers, used as refuges for the clergy in time of Viking invasion, which are so characteristic a feature of the later Irish church. The older of the two appears to be the round tower at Brechin, which stands at the south-west corner of the thirteenth-century cathedral church, to which it is now joined. To the base of the spire, a fourteenth-century addition, the tower measures 86 feet 9 inches in height, and it is 7 feet 11 inches in internal basal diameter, the wall here being 3 feet 8 inches thick. Wooden floors divided the interior into seven storeys. The masonry is of large red sandstone blocks, wrought to the curve but not regularly coursed, and occasionally with joggled or interlocking joints. There are two original windows, with flat heads and inclined jambs, in the Celtic manner. Equally Celtic is the doorway, which is placed about 12 feet above the original ground level. It has inclined jambs and an arched head cut in a single stone. All round the margin of the door runs a raised band with pellet enrichment, thoroughly Irish in character, and over the arch is a Crucifixion, shown in the Irish fashion, with our Saviour's legs uncrossed. On either side are clerics, one carrying the characteristic *bachuill* or curved pastoral staff, while the other has a tau-cross, a very ancient form. At the foot of the doorway crouch two grotesque beasts, while at its upper end are two blank projecting blocks of stone, doubtless intended to be similarly carved. The doorway is 6 feet 7½ inches in height. This tower was probably built soon after 990, when King Kenneth II MacMaelcholuim is recorded to have 'given to the Lord the great monastery of Brechin.' This act is generally understood to have implied the handing over of an ancient Pictish centre to the Columban or Scotic clergy, who would naturally thereafter build, in a district peculiarly exposed to the Danish ravagings, a round tower of the type familiar in the Irish birthland of their Church. If the word of a late mediaeval historian may be trusted, the tower is known to have been in existence in the year 1012.

The Abernethy round tower—a 'stately hollow pillar,' as old Sandy Gordon quaintly described it in 1728—stands on the edge of the ancient churchyard. It is 72 feet in height and 8 feet in basal diameter, within walls 3 feet 6 inches thick. In the interior were six stages of wooden floors. The tower is well built of coursed masonry. The lower courses—reaching to a height of about 14 feet —are of hard grey freestone in oblong blocks; but thereafter the tower is built in cubical, wide-jointed buff-coloured freestone ashlar of pronouncedly Romanesque type. In both sections the stones are wrought to the curved outline of the tower. The doorway, which is encircled by a raised band, has inclined jambs in the Irish style, and an arched head cut out of a single stone. It is now about 3 feet above ground level. The window in the second storey also has inclined jambs, and a triangular head cut out of one stone. The uppermost windows, four in number, show Irish influence persisting in their inclined jambs, but the nook shafts and arch moulds are of distinctly Romanesque design. It is clear that the greater part of the tower has been rebuilt, probably about the end of the eleventh century, when Norman influence was making itself felt.

The stump of a third round tower still exists at Iona, close west of the present Cathedral or Benedictine Abbey. The site of the Columban monastery was about a quarter of a mile farther to the north. Probably it was shifted to the southern position at the time, about 814-18, when it seems to have been rebuilt in stone after the Viking invasions. This would appear to be proved by the presence, in association with the Benedictine ruins, of remains belonging to an earlier monastery, apparently of late Irish type: namely, in addition to the round tower aforesaid, a small church immediately north of the Cathedral choir, a large building farther to the north which may have been the refectory, the curious little chamber at the north-west corner of the Cathedral nave, and other traces. The small church and oratory are oriented, whereas the Benedictine Abbey is deflected widely to the south. There is good reason for believing that the little chamber at the north-west corner of the Benedictine nave enclosed the shrine of Columba.

To the west end of the little chancelled church on the island of Egilsey, in the Orkneys, is attached a round tower, corresponding more or less, in general appearance, to the Irish pattern, but it is evidently of contemporary build with the church, and it is doubtful whether the latter is really of the high antiquity to which it is usually assigned.

33 The Cathedral and St. Oran's Chapel, Iona

34 View from the East

35 The Cloister

THE ABBEY BUILDINGS ON THE ISLAND OF INCHCOLM IN THE FIRTH OF FORTH

The remarkable round church at Orphir, also in Orkney, with its semicircular apse, appears to be of Romanesque date, and certainly owes nothing to a Celtic tradition.

The historian Bede tells us that in 710 Nechtan Macderile, King of the Picts, wrote to Ceolfrid, the Anglian abbot of the monastery of St. Peter at Wearmouth, craving information as to the points wherein Roman practice differed from that which had grown up in the Celtic Church during the period when the Teutonic invasions had sundered it from the rest of Christendom; and asking also, 'that architects should be sent to him to make a church of stone among his people after the manner of the Romans, promising to dedicate it in honour of the prince of the Apostles.' St. Boniface, the missionary whom Ceolfrid despatched, was quartered for some time at Restennet in Angus: and here, incorporated in the ruins of the later Augustinian house—dedicated to St. Peter—is the lower part of a square tower of very early Romanesque work, the details of which do not exclude the possibility that it may be a veritable remnant of the church erected by the Northumbrian masons in the reign of King Nechtan. The south door, with its arch cut out of a single stone, and wrought with a raised band or margin, and the east tower arch, with its tilted or wedged up and irregularly tailed voussoirs, have much affinity with Saxon work.

In Gaul, and later on in South Britain, Celtic civilisation received its death-blow from the Roman conquest, which submerged the native arts and crafts in the general uniformitarian culture of the Latin west. But in Pictland and in Ireland, both of which remained outwith the sphere of Rome, the native Celtic culture continued to flourish right down into the Middle Ages. So far as the Scottish Lowlands are concerned, Latin civilisation triumphed over its Celtic predecessor as a result of the Norman penetration in the twelfth century, which brought the lovely art of the sculptured stones to an end. But in the Highlands and the Western Isles Celtic art continued to flourish, and to blossom in new forms of beauty, throughout the mediaeval period, and was only extinguished finally by the Reformation. These late West Highland crosses and grave-slabs, now for the most part overgrown and neglected, offer a fruitful field of study. The crosses are usually free-standing, after the Irish fashion, and have a solid disc in place of the halo or ring of glory found at an earlier period. Alongside the older Celtic decorative patterns, elements derived from mediaeval art, such as the vine scroll and other form of foliage, become frequent. Representations of the Crucifixion, seldom found in earlier Celtic art, are now quite common. Grotesque figure sculpture remains in use, and is usually executed with surprising vigour. The grave-slabs—again in the Irish manner—are recumbent, and often show figures of warriors clad in the peculiar chain and quilted armour of the Western Highlands. With these crosses and grave-slabs, many of which were carved in the years immediately preceding the Reformation, the long and brilliant history of Celtic monumental art in Scotland comes to a close.

G. P. H. Watson
F.R.I.B.A.

~~~~~~

THE
CHURCH IN MEDIAEVAL SCOTLAND

~~~~~~

WHEN the Western Church came to be refashioned and systematised towards the end of the eleventh century by Hildebrand, who was called to the Papacy as Gregory VII, Scotland, then at the extreme north-western corner of Christendom, fell into line with the movement in more central regions through the influence of the saintly Margaret, Queen of Malcolm Canmore. It was no new thing for a consort to interest herself in ecclesiastical politics. The mission of Paulinus to Northumbria at the end of the sixth century owed its success mainly to the wife of King Edwin. The wife of Osway, King of the same province, turned her husband's allegiance from Iona to Rome in the century following. Four centuries later, Queen Margaret similarly shook her husband's faith in the efficiency of the Celtic Church, which, indeed, seems to have been reactionary and unable to adapt itself to the conditions of a rapidly changing world. Her firm understanding and her grasp of ecclesiastical affairs were inherited by her sons.

To King David I must be given credit for setting up in Scotland a fabric of Church and State sufficiently stable to last throughout the Middle Ages. By the close of his reign, or shortly after, the country had already been divided into parishes, each with its own church and priest, grouped for administrative purposes into dioceses, nine of them purely Scottish, with two others respectively under the jurisdiction of York and Hamburg; two additional sees were erected subsequently. King David, moreover, like his immediate predecessors, had foreseen the advantage of encouraging the immigration of colonies of religious, monks and canons from abroad; with the latter class he sought to merge the autonomous elements in the Celtic clergy, having realised the danger of neglecting vested interests. Thus, when he died in 1153, Scotland was already studded with ecclesiastical buildings, a nucleus that later generations were to enlarge and adorn.

The first parishes corresponded roughly to the larger estates. When these manors came to be divided up in course of time, a chapel was commonly built for convenience upon each of the smaller portions. Such chapels were at first under the jurisdiction of the parent parish church, but in the end, many, if not the majority of them, came to enjoy full parochial rights. Thus, at the advent of the Reformation, there were no fewer than nine hundred and twenty-four parish churches, apart from those in Argyll, for which no figures are available. This increase in the number of parish churches was accompanied by an expansion of the religious communities. In the year 1207, for instance, there were only thirty-six houses of monks and canons. By the end of the fifteenth century the number had risen to eighty-six, if the nunneries be included.

The heyday of monasticism in Scotland fell in the thirteenth century. Monastic life, with its objective outlook, gradually began to lose its appeal and then gave ground before the non-capitalist Franciscan movement. In 1231 the friars crossed the Tweed and eventually built up forty communities. Then, from the close of the fourteenth century onwards, it became customary for rich trade-guilds and wealthy landowners to found Collegiate churches: churches, that is to say, served by a body of clergy known as a college, in which the canonical services might be celebrated more fully than was possible in the ordinary parish church, and in which the anniversaries of the founders and their kin might be fittingly commemorated. Such churches, numbering about forty in all, were in a sense glorified chantries.

The classifications thus briefly outlined reflect an elaborate and highly organised ecclesiastical system based upon Rome, a system

36 St. Rule's Tower, St. Andrews, with the ruins of the Gothic Cathedral

ST. MAGNUS' CATHEDRAL, KIRKWALL, ORKNEY

however, that has left fewer monuments than might be expected. The comparative rarity of mediaeval church architecture in Scotland is due to three main causes: war, the Reformation, and neglect, the last being the most potent factor. As far back as the year 1242 the Bishop of St. Andrews had occasion to admonish his clergy to uphold their churches properly on pain of suspension of their stipends. And as the Reformation loomed ahead matters became progressively worse. Time and again abbots, provosts, and deans were exhorted to repair their churches, no easy matter when revenues were consistently falling. War, however, at all times took heavy toll of churches, especially in the regions south of the Forth, the Border abbeys, in particular, falling an easy prey to the English invader. As for the Reformation, while such abbeys, friaries, and other religious houses as refused to accept Protestant principles were certainly 'dung doun,' the vast majority of the Scottish churches were merely 'cleansed'; in some cases, indeed, the church plate was sold and the proceeds applied to the fabric fund. When the Reformation had become an accomplished fact many parish churches were found to be redundant, and the number was thereupon reduced to six hundred, grouped in fifty-three presbyteries.

Of the churches built in Scotland for the Roman rite the oldest survivor must be the diminutive chapel of St. Margaret, which commands the Capital from the apex of the Castle rock. Here Queen Margaret worshipped and heard her final Mass, passing thence to her death-bed in 1093. This tiny cell, in which marriages and baptisms are still occasionally celebrated, may, in a sense, be said to be the mother of our parish and collegiate churches. But the passage of eight and a half centuries have necessarily taken toll of the fabric, which shows obvious signs of renewal and repair. Thus, the chancel-arch now seen was provided by King David I to replace an earlier screen, along with the semi-dome covering the sanctuary. The south wall had to be underpinned in the sixteenth century, when the surface of an adjoining roadway was lowered, and the nave is not only entered today through a modern doorway but is covered with a modern barrel vault.

An equally high antiquity, however, may be assigned to a fragment at Orphir in Orkney, all that is left of the only round church to be built in the area comprising the Scotland of today. This was probably copied directly from a Baltic model. But alien forms did not oust the native all at once—survivals of Celtic church architecture can still be seen in the round towers at Abernethy and Brechin. And contemporary square towers serving a similar purpose of belfry combined with watch-tower are still to the fore at Muthill and Dunblane. From the point of view of fine architecture, however, undoubtedly the most interesting of the early Scottish churches is that of St. Regulus, the first church of the Augustinian priory at St. Andrews, which can be dated with some certainty to the years between 1125 and 1144. Its masonry is so similar to that of a church belonging to the same Order at Wharram-le-Street as to suggest that some, at least, of the masons came directly from Yorkshire to Fife. On the other hand, the architectural detail has an even closer parallel in the abbey church of Aubazine near Limoges, which was founded in 1135. St. Regulus' church had a high, unaisled, and unvaulted choir, with a sanctuary, probably square-ended, and a lofty, square, western tower. A nave was added at some later time. While nave and sanctuary have perished, the other parts are entire but for their roofs. The fabric is exceptionally well built, and it lacks the surface ornament with which most churches of this time are accented. For effect it relies solely on mass and proportion.

This church, it must be remembered, was the cathedral of St. Andrews until some time after 1160, when a more sumptuous fabric took its place. The contemporary cathedral of Moray was no more elaborate. As a general rule, the first church to be built for a given monastery or diocese in the first half of the twelfth century was of modest dimensions and simple architecture, in some cases of timber construction and in at least one instance of clay; when funds accrued for extension the primary building was invariably scrapped. Yet, on the other hand, the first cathedral in the Orkneys, built at Birsay in 1050, seems to have been both cruciform and apsidal-ended, while its successor, St. Magnus' cathedral at Kirkwall, which was founded in 1137, was intended from the outset to be a fully developed cruciform, aisled church of three storeys, with western and central towers and an apsidal sanctuary.

But even St. Magnus' itself is small for a church of the first rank, if judged by southern and Continental standards. Yet the proportions are so happy that it appears to be much larger than it actually is, one proof that the architect was skilled in his profession. There is, indeed, nothing unsophisticated about the design, which, generally, suggests the work of the Durham school; the homeland of Norway, it should be remembered, had to draw upon English, French, and German masons in constructing her own Christ-kirks. Three and a half centuries passed ere St. Magnus' cathedral was completed, and in that space of time various departures were made from the original scheme. The western towers, for instance, were omitted, to the detriment of the structure. Then the crossing was reconstructed bodily towards the end of the twelfth century, and the apse was removed in the century following to make way for an eastward extension of the choir. Such an extension, due to the desire for greater privacy on the part of the clergy, was quite normal in the thirteenth century. Indeed, the only major twelfth-century churches that retain their original east ends are the cathedral church of 1160 at St. Andrews and the almost contemporary abbey church of Arbroath. The primary work at Kirkwall is virile and dignified, while the thirteenth-century additions achieve real distinction. The apse and the aisles were designed for rib-vaulting, while the major spans were intended to have open timber roofs. Such was the general practice in Scotland until the fourteenth century.

The work of the Durham school is even more evident in the nave of the Benedictine abbey church of Dunfermline. Built between 1128 and 1150 as an aisled, cruciform building with central and western towers, this replaced an earlier church, founded about 1070 by Queen Margaret, vestiges of which can still be seen beneath the floor of this, its successor. It has come down as our finest specimen of Scoto-Norman major architecture, although the choir and transepts had to be built anew in 1819, having long been ruinous. The interior of the nave has real grandeur and exemplifies the placidity and strength of Romanesque design at its best. Unlike Dunfermline, which rose rapidly, few large churches were completed within a generation. Progress depended both on the funds available and on the activity of the promoters of the enterprise. A generous patron and an energetic abbot made for speed. But, even in the most favourable circumstances, building was slow work in

F

the Middle Ages. For one thing, it was no easy matter to procure suitable materials. The means of preparing and transporting them were primitive. But if material was difficult to come by, labour was relatively cheap, and consequently each individual piece of material was carefully selected for its special purpose and carefully and fully wrought. All this took time. And in such circumstances it is not surprising to find that the church of the Augustinian abbey of Jedburgh, founded in 1147, took over three-quarters of a century to build. But this was a much more ambitious structure than its sister church, St. Regulus'. A cruciform-aisled building, it had apsidioles on the eastern sides of the transepts and the high, square presbytery usual in churches of the Augustinian and Cistercian Orders. The choir and transepts were completed as a unit in the earlier phase of Romanesque architecture. Then the nave was built from the west gable eastward in the Transitional and early Gothic development current at the turn of the twelfth and thirteenth centuries, and here, as elsewhere, that particular fusion of styles has produced an exquisite structure, entirely unselfconscious. The western façade is the only Transitional frontispiece standing comparatively intact in Scotland. The east end was extended in the thirteenth century. The choir arcade, which is the earliest part of all, is of special interest, since it rises to include the triforium storey and permits an adequate pier arcade in combination with a comparatively low wall-head. This arrangement is unique in Scotland, but in England two Benedictine and two Augustinian churches have a generally similar form of bay design; generally, if the triforium is united to another storey, the clearstorey is the one preferred.

In the church of the neighbouring abbey of Kelso, built for Tironensians who had removed here from Selkirk in 1128, the older types of Romanesque ornament may be seen grafted upon the new Transitional forms. All that survives is the late twelfth-century west end, incomplete at that. And the plan as a whole was a puzzle to ecclesiologists until recently when attention was drawn to a sixteenth-century description of the place, which made it clear that Kelso, like Ely and Bury St. Edmund's, had western transepts as well as a western crossing tower and a Galilee, a layout indicative of Teutonic influence. The part in best preservation

39 The Nave and Tower

40 The Nave looking East (thirteenth century)

JEDBURGH ABBEY, ROXBURGHSHIRE

41 Leuchars Church, Fife. The chancel is Norman, the tower
seventeenth century

42 Romanesque Doorway, Dalmeny Church, Midlothian.   The most
complete Norman church in Scotland

43 Nave, Dunfermline Abbey, Fife. Showing the massive Norman
piers, two of them with chevron and spiral ornament

is the north transept, an entirely admirable composition, although capped by a seventeenth-century gable-head. Whether intentional or not, the interior must have appeared quite dramatic, looking from the long, dark nave into brilliantly lit transepts at either end. Throughout the building the surfaces are richly arcaded, and the horizontal lines of the pier arcades contrast agreeably with tiers of vertical arcading in the transepts and Galilee.

Summing up the characteristics of the major churches erected at the time of the Norman penetration, one may say that they were massive, aisled, cruciform buildings, apsidal-ended if built in the first half of the twelfth century and square-ended if built later. All had central towers, western towers were less common. The dominant lines were horizontal, although the bay design was three-storeyed. Only the aisles and the apses were intended to be vaulted, and for such vaults the external abutment provided was shallow. Piers were either cylindrical or square, with capitals cushion-shaped when not moulded, conventional foliaceous carving only coming into vogue in the latter part of the century. Arches were round. Doorways were elaborate, invariably built in several orders, usually enriched with repeating patterns. Windows were small, for glass had not yet come into common use. Arches, window-heads, and stringcourses were enriched with conventional ornament—chevrons, billets, damiers, chip-carved patterns and the like. The lower part of the internal walls was decorated with arcading, while the whole of the internal wall-surfaces received a thin coat of plaster as a ground for painted patterns or allegorical pictures. The outside of the walls was probably lime-washed.

As for the minor churches of the time such as served the parishes, the finest are to be seen at Dalmeny and Leuchars, while there is an interesting series in Orkney and Shetland, the church of St. Magnus on the island of Egilsay being specially notable. But Romanesque buildings are not uncommon in other parts, re-dressed and expanded to meet later requirements. Dalmeny church, dating from about 1160, has a west tower, recently renewed, with nave, chancel, and sanctuary, the last in the form of a stilted apse. The windows, set in the upper part of the walls, have nook-shafts supporting round arch-heads enriched with chevron ornament. The doorway, sur-mounted by an intersecting arcade, also has nook-shafts to support the arch-head, which originally enclosed a sculptured tympanum, such as may be seen at Linton church in Roxburgh. The voussoirs are carved with subjects taken from Bestiaries and other sources. The nave had an open timber roof, but the other parts were and still are rib-vaulted. The vaulting-ribs of the chancel and the arches which open to the chancel and to the sanctuary are all heavily enriched with chevrons.

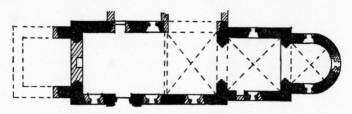

Dalmeny Church

10   0   10   20   30   40   50 *Feet*

At Leuchars church, built between 1183 and 1187, the nave is modern, and of the original fabric there remains only the chancel and the apsidal sanctuary, the latter crowned with a seventeenth-century bell-turret. The architectural membrane is even more richly treated than at Dalmeny. The walls are clad externally with continuous arcades, every alternate bay of the upper tier containing a narrow window. The chancel-arch is enriched with a damier pattern, while that of the sanctuary is ornamented with billets. The sanctuary is vaulted, but only the eastern part of the vault is ribbed. Even more ornate than either of these churches was another at Tynninghame, East Lothian, if one may judge from the fragment that has survived. To the ecclesiologist its special interest is the provision for additional altars on either side of the chancel-arch.

In contrast to their southern contemporaries the parish churches in Orkney and Shetland are modest buildings indeed, partly because the local flagstone and limestone are unsuitable for fine mason-work or for moulding or carving. Even for their time they are

44 Church of the Holy Rude, Stirling

45 The Abbey, Holyrood, Edinburgh

46 Dundrennan Abbey, Galloway

47 Dryburgh Abbey, Berwickshire

archaic in appearance. For example, their arches are set back from the face of the pier to allow the constructural centering to rest on the impost, a method used in Saxon and Celtic work and found even in some Roman buildings. Like many East Anglian buildings, St. Magnus' church on Egilsay has a lofty round tower attached to the west end of the nave and a square chancel with a room above its vault. And like many of its neighbours it has no proper chancel-arch, the end of the chancel-vault serving instead. The doors and windows are quite undistinguished. Nevertheless, this building has the quality of vitality and is the more impressive on account of its stark simplicity.

As the twelfth century drew to its close, experiments made in design and construction prepared the way for the glory of Gothic architecture. And Scotland shared in the general advance, if sometimes lagging a little behind. Buildings became lighter. Round arch gave way to pointed, and the forms, generally, became elongated, for the quality of slenderness was now much admired. Vertical instead of horizontal accents began to be stressed. The composition became unified. The structure became articulated. Mouldings and shaftings tended to become detached from the structure, in appearance if not in reality.

In the history of mediaeval architecture the Transitional period, when Romanesque design develops into Gothic, is regarded as one of the greatest on account of the aesthetic value of its product. And in Scotland no finer piece of Transitional or early Gothic work took shape than the nave at Holyrood, virtually all that remains of this Augustinian abbey founded by King David I. Although of moderate size, this nave, begun at the turn of the twelfth and thirteenth centuries, is accepted as one of our major monuments. The tradition that French or Flemish masons were employed in the early stages of the work is borne out by the evidence of the architectural detail. This was the first large church in Scotland intended to be vaulted throughout. The high vault, although it was not constructed before 1260, had been projected from the first. As it finally took shape it was sexpartite, a form that led inevitably to duality in the design of the whole superstructure. The façade of Holyrood, extended by means of towers attached to the corners of the aisles, is very rich and has real grandeur. Its central features are a distinguished west doorway, which King Charles I did his best to mutilate, and a great six-light window above, formerly surmounted by eight bays of arcading in the upper part of the gable. The west window contains a tribune from which the hymn 'Glory, Laud and Honour' was sung on Palm Sunday. And the rest of the façade is richly arcaded. One may, indeed, say that an air of sophisticated elegance pervades this building.

Although the choir of Holyrood has vanished, at Coldingham one can still see the east end of a contemporary Benedictine priory church, the west and south sides of which were rebuilt about 1855. There the walls are divided into bays by buttresses which are still mere pilaster-strips in the early Romanesque tradition. Each bay contains arcading in the lower part and a pointed window in the upper one. The plan is oblong and unaisled. The triforium has been omitted as a separate storey, possibly following Cistercian practice, which began about this time to influence the architecture of other Orders, of the Premonstratensians and of the Tironensians in particular.

There is no very close correspondence, however, with contemporary Cistercian work in the architecture of the Tironensian abbey at Arbroath, which may be referred to the first decade of the thirteenth century. The aisled, cruciform church has certainly eastern transeptal chapels and a high, unaisled presbytery, but there were two western towers in addition to one at the crossing. The only parts vaulted were the aisles and, possibly, the presbytery. The buttresses, it may be added, are no longer mere pilaster-strips but have considerable projection. The east end is dilapidated, yet enough is left to indicate that it expressed the internal ordinance. The day of the unified eastern façade had not yet come. At Arbroath the south transept is the part best preserved, and its tall lancets, set over tiers of arcading, faintly reminiscent of the sister church at Kelso, still rise through two storeys, above which they were surmounted by that favourite feature of the time, a great circular light. And the west front, incomplete as it stands, is not without interest. The central feature is, necessarily, the west doorway, here heavily recessed within a tunnel of masonry, the substructure of a great projecting porch. This porch had two storeys, the upper one a tribune, as at Holyrood and St. Andrews. From the roof of

48　Lincluden College, Galloway

49　The Nave, Dunblane Cathedral, Perthshire

51 Exterior of the Chancel

50 North Wall of the Choir

COLDINGHAM PRIORY, BERWICKSHIRE

53 Arbroath Abbey, Angus

52 Aisle, Arbuthnott Church, Kincardineshire

54 Elgin Cathedral. Founded 1224

the porch rose arcading, while the whole upper part of the gable was occupied by a great circular light.

In the century that saw so many important buildings started, fashions in architecture passed rapidly and without material change from one end of the kingdom to the other. Even in so remote a quarter as Lorn a Transitional chapel was erected at Dunstaffnage comparable to anything that rose nearer the main stream of the artistic current. This little building is oblong and single-chambered, for the chancel was only separated from the nave by a timber screen. Its end and side windows, however, were so grouped as to make a distinction between the two parts. And the altar was no doubt elevated to define the sanctuary. This chapel seems to be one of the first to be built upon this type of plan, which was to hold good for many of the smaller churches of the thirteenth and fourteenth centuries.

To the Transitional period may also be ascribed the churches of the Cistercian abbeys at Dundrennan and Glenluce in Galloway. That of Glenluce is very incomplete, although the whole plan has recently been recovered by excavation. But enough is left at Dundrennan to show what the Cistercians were able to build in the very flower of their energy. The plan is orthodox, aisled nave, transepts with eastern chapel aisles, and a high unaisled presbytery. The bay design is austere, but is unusual in having a triforium storey, which appears as a blind arcade in the north transept and as an open arcade in the southern one. The only parts vaulted were the presbytery and the aisles. As for the architecture generally, it shows close attention to significant form. And the front of the chapter-house, splendid even in its ruin, has been an exceptional example of fine thirteenth-century design.

The church of the Premonstratensian abbey at Dryburgh, which was probably modelled upon another at Talley in Carmarthenshire, is more advanced in style. Dating from the beginning of the thirteenth century, it is cruciform, with a short, aisled nave, transepts with eastern chapels, and a high, unaisled presbytery with side chapels in échelon, the most graceful of eastern endings. The bay design, seen complete only at the junction of the north transept and the presbytery, shows an alternative solution of the problem noticed at Jedburgh. Here the triforium has been reduced in height. Above the crossing rose a low bell-tower, which was vaulted above the crossing arches, a rare occurrence at so early a time. The west end was rebuilt after 1385, the year in which the abbey was destroyed by the English, but apart from its west doorway it is as fragmentary as the rest. The doorway, however, is intact, and its round arch, enriched with paterae, shows the reversion to Romanesque forms current in Scotland in and about the fifteenth century.

So many churches were founded in the twelfth century that the primary needs of the community were met for some time to come. And much of the thirteenth-century work consisted of completion and extension. For instance, in 1224, when Bricius Douglas, bishop of Moray, elected to transfer his seat from Spynie to Elgin, the Transitional church of Holy Trinity at Elgin was enlarged and completed to become the cathedral of his diocese. As it had been laid out towards the close of the twelfth century this had comprised an aisled nave with unaisled transepts and presbytery, and western and central towers, the eastern towers being the only parts vaulted. The three eastern bays of the nave south aisle were now extended southwards to provide additional accommodation. A disastrous fire in 1270 prepared the way for a major reconstruction. The nave was now provided with double aisles in the French fashion, while the eastern limb was extended to twice its former length and given a vaulted aisle on each side, a passage from the northern one leading to an octagonal chapter-house. In 1390 the cathedral was burnt by the Wolf of Badenoch, but the damage was made good, and at the Reformation Elgin was considered to be quite the finest of all the Scottish cathedrals, a circumstance that did not prevent its lapsing into ruin, the bishop of the time having paved the way for its dilapidation by alienating its revenues. Even as it stands today this church is full of interest to all who can appreciate fine detail and proportion, the east end in particular being a work of inspired genius. The gable rises high and sheer within its corner turrets and has two tiers of lofty lancets, exquisitely enriched, and a rose window in the upper part of the gable. The great west doorway, moreover, is one of the finest in the country.

The bishop of Glasgow, like his colleague of Moray, seems to have started to rebuild an earlier church as his cathedral about the second quarter of the thirteenth century. But he incorporated a

55 Glasgow Cathedral.   The Cathedral is the largest and best preserved
Gothic structure in Scotland

57 The Nave

56 The Crypt

GLASGOW CATHEDRAL

mere fragment of the old building and laid out a virtually new church upon a plan novel to Scotland, although already firmly established in the south. This type of plan, arranged in the first instance with an eye to the pilgrim industry, not only gave a complete ambulatory with greater chapel space, but also made for simpler and more direct construction. The site was uneven, a circumstance taken advantage of to provide a crypt for the shrine of St. Mungo, the patron saint. Altogether the arrangement of this church shows a radical departure from the monastic plan of the major churches previously mentioned. It provided an aisled nave and aisled presbytery with rudimentary transepts projecting no farther than the limits of the aisles. There were towers at the crossing and at the western corners, but the latter were removed less than a century ago, leaving the principal façade mutilated and without focus. The high wall-heads, which were not designed for vaulting, still support fine fourteenth-century timber roofs, that of the nave an open roof with tie-beams, while the choir roof, or foiled section, is boarded and ribbed. Steps still lead from the crossing to the crypt below the choir. The walls of the crypt are carried up for the choir aisles, the choir arcade and its high wall-heads rising within. Thus, instead of the sheer east end seen at Elgin, one finds at Glasgow the ending known as 'squared peri-apsidal,' the British equivalent of the French chevet. The nave of Glasgow came under construction at the turn of the thirteenth and fourteenth centuries, the crossing tower at the beginning of the century following. Then an aisle was thrown out some time after 1484 in extension of the south transept, but at a lower level. One of the major features of the cathedral is the crypt and its vault, altogether an exceptional piece of design and construction. The provision of a central pier upon the axis of the plan is rare for Scotland, while the pulpitum is a rare survival from the fifteenth century.

In the cathedral church of Dunblane, started about a quarter of a century after Glasgow, an even simpler plan was adopted comprising an aisled nave, which incorporates the Romanesque tower previously mentioned, and a long presbytery with a lateral chapel aisle running along most of the north side. The bay design is particularly fine and includes a very rich pier arcade surmounted by a superb clearstorey arcade. The triforium storey has been

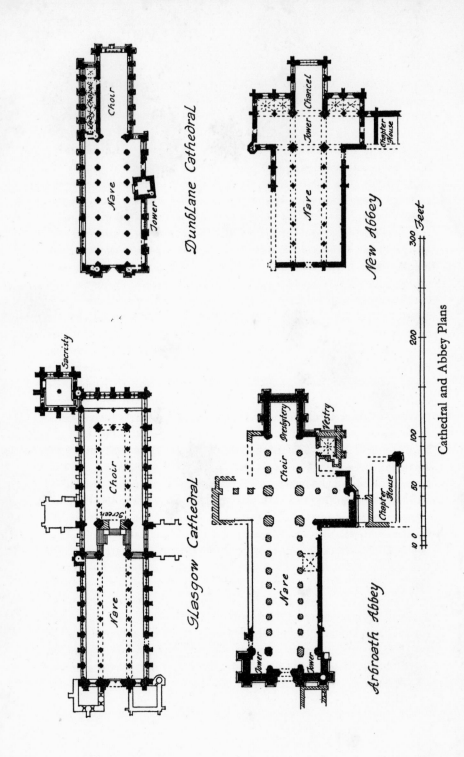

Dunblane Cathedral

New Abbey

Glasgow Cathedral

Arbroath Abbey

Cathedral and Abbey Plans

10 0   50   100   200   300 Feet

suppressed. The east and west ends, moreover, which date respectively from the middle of the thirteenth and the beginning of the century following, are amongst the ablest works of their time. Dunblane, apparently, was the source of inspiration for the little mid-twelfth-century priory church of Austin canons, so romantically situated on Inchmahome on the Lake of Menteith. This has an unaisled presbytery and a short nave with an aisle on its north side which abuts on a western tower. The tower, however, was rebuilt after the rest had been completed. At the sister abbey of Cambuskenneth, on the other hand, the fine thirteenth-century tower still stands intact, although the church beside it which rose has perished.

The later cathedral church of St. Andrews has been mentioned in passing. Once the greatest church in all Scotland, it is represented today by a mere vestige. When complete, it was an aisled cruciform structure with a central tower and a high unaisled presbytery. The nave arcade was fourteen bays in length until the west gable was blown down about 1275 and was thereupon rebuilt two bays farther east. Even then the nave remained the longest in the country. The west front as rebuilt was screened by a great vaulted porch, the most elaborate of three in Scotland. The east gable underwent alteration in the fifteenth century.

The architecture of the thirteenth century differed considerably from what went before. In the first place, the choir arm tended to lengthen and was invariably square-ended. Then church plans were arranged with a view to accommodating additional altars. As for the structure, this became compacted and less massy. The wall or solid began to give way to the void as the part of paramount importance. As for the windows themselves, slender lancets came into fashion and were at first spaced far apart. Then they were grouped together and, finally, they were enclosed within an outer arch. The bay design became markedly vertical. The triforium became less important and was ultimately omitted. Thereupon the clearstorey invariably opened to a passage. The round arch was quite obsolete and had been replaced by a pointed one with archivolts built in three orders, subdivided by small mouldings that became increasingly intricate as the century advanced. As the piers became higher and more slender they came to be composed of circular and keel-shaped shafts worked round a central core in the majority of cases. Some, however, were octagonal. The bases were profiled with rounds, fillets, and deeply undercut hollows. The capitals had round abaci with rounded mouldings, the upper member deeply undercut, while the bell below was concave and either simply moulded or enriched with stiff trefoil foliage.

The parish churches of the time were simple enough, to judge by the survivals. Some, like Prestonkirk, Burntisland, and Kinghorn, consisted of nave and chancel, but the majority were oblong, with no more than a screen to separate the chancel from the nave. Of the latter may be instanced a late example at Temple, which first belonged to the Templars, and then to the Hospitallers after 1312. After the Wars of Independence Scotland was too exhausted in purse and spirit to raise new foundations for some considerable time. Any building that was done in the first half of the fourteenth century was more in the way of completion and necessary rebuilding. And it is significant that Scots designers now part company with their English colleagues and look more often to the Continent for inspiration. In the latter part of the century, when church building resumed its normal course, it was no longer instigated mainly by prelate or abbot, but by the friar, the smaller landowner, and the burgher class, definite evidence that a social change was taking place. But there is one important foundation at least to be reported. At the turn of the thirteenth and fourteenth centuries the Cistercians built a new abbey in Galloway, Dulce Cor, or Sweetheart as it is familiarly known. The foundation was made in 1273 by the Lady Devorgilla to perpetuate the memory of her husband, John Balliol of Barnard Castle. The layout follows the usual Cistercian lines, aisled nave, transepts with eastern chapels, and an unaisled presbytery. The aisles and chapels were the only parts vaulted. While the triforium has been omitted from the bay design, above the crossing rises a tower of decidedly secular aspect. The architecture generally is in step with contemporary work in the south, but national characteristics will be found on close inspection.

Reference must also be made to the reconstruction of Paisley abbey. This Cluniac house was founded in 1160, its church being modelled upon that of Cerisy in France. It was burned by the English in 1307. What survived the fire was patched up pending

58 Sweetheart Abbey, Galloway (thirteenth and fourteenth centuries)

59 St. Monan's Church, Fife (late fourteenth century)

60 Crichton Church, Midlothian.   Built by Sir William Crichton in 1449

61　View from North-West, with Cloister Court in foreground

62　From South-West

MELROSE ABBEY, ROXBURGHSHIRE

64 Font, Inverkeithing Church, Fife

63 The fifteenth-century vaulting in the Chapter
House of Elgin Cathedral

the accumulation of funds for rebuilding. Forward from the close of the fourteenth century it was reconstructed as a cruciform church with an aisled nave, the work taking the best part of a century to complete. Soon after the rebuilding was finished the crossing tower fell and wrecked the eastern arm. Of the primary work there remains the lower part of the west front and part of the south aisle. The nave, as reconstructed, is one of the major accomplishments of Scottish fourteenth-century architecture, and its bay design is of special interest for the triforium is corbelled out round the piers, as at Rouen, to avoid interference with their stability. The clearstorey above has two pointed windows in each bay, copied, apparently, from older work.

Another extensive reconstruction was carried out in the parish church of St. Giles in Edinburgh. This, in the first instance, was a Romanesque building, presumably of nave and chancel, of which the only vestige is a solitary cushion-capital built into the present fabric. It is not unreasonable to suppose that the chancel was extended in the thirteenth century. However that may be, the growing importance of the burgh in the fourteenth century led to the provision of aisles, five bays long, on each side of the nave. A tower, moreover, was contemplated at the north-west corner, but that particular project was abandoned in favour of a central tower abutted by rudimentary transepts, as at Glasgow. The burgh was thrice ravaged by the English in the fourteenth century and its church did not pass unscathed. In 1385 Richard II gave it to the flames, and their traces were still visible upon the crossing piers within living memory. Even so, a substantial part of the fabric must have escaped serious damage, since the Town Council were in a position to add five vaulted chapels beyond the nave south aisle in two years' time. When these were completed, about 1391, a corresponding series of chapels was added to the north side. Then the eastern arm was rebuilt with aisles of four bays and the whole was vaulted, the bays first built being highly domical. About 1453 the eastern arm was lengthened by one bay and its wall-heads were raised to accommodate a clearstorey. The existing high vault of the choir had thereupon to come down and was replaced by the fine tierceron vault now seen. The north transept was next extended. Then in 1454 an aisle of three bays was thrown out beyond the south choir aisle. In 1466 the ambitions of the citizens were realised and their church was raised to collegiate status, thirty years after their application had first been made. But the work of reconstruction continued for half a century longer. Some time before the Reformation the south transept in its turn had been extended and a chantry chapel had been added on each side of it. Finally the crossing tower was capped with an open crown spire, a feature almost peculiar to Scotland. Such was the fabric, a homespun fabric owing nothing to outside aid, that underwent a drastic restoration in 1829, leaving the outside a mere *pastiche*. The interior, however, is still impressive and remarkably harmonious considering its chequered history. The chapel piers are unusually graceful and have finely carved capitals, while the vaulting is exceptionally good for a parish church.

Of the smaller churches built in the fourteenth century one of the best, from an architectural point of view, stands at St. Monan's in Fife. This had been laid out in 1362 as an aisle-less cruciform building but the nave was never built. Over the crossing rises a tower with a parapet and a low spire; the superstructure, however, dates only from the sixteenth century and replaces an original broach spire. The fenestration of this church is interesting. Most of the windows have the flowing tracery current at this time, but the lights of the south transept hark back to plate tracery, a much earlier form which was long out of date when this church was built. When the fabric was restored in 1828 the floor was lowered between three and four feet. The internal proportions are thereby changed, but the chancel with its fine ribbed vault is otherwise intact and forms an interesting link between the earlier and later mediaeval churches. Then at Barevan, near Cawdor, one can still see the ruin of a little oblong parish church of 'Dunstaffnage' type which was divided by the chancel screen into two almost equal parts. And reference must also be made to two other late fourteen-century churches, both in Lanarkshire and dedicated alike to St. Bride. The earlier of the pair, at Douglas, represents the reconstruction of an older fabric. Little more survives than the south aisle of the nave and the oblong unaisled choir. Architecturally undistinguished, this eastern arm contains three fine altar tombs. The other church, situated at Bothwell, was founded in 1398 by

Archibald the Grim, third Earl of Douglas, as a collegiate establishment. Its oblong choir seems to have been the only part built. The walls are divided into bays by buttresses with sloping tops. Every bay, save one from which the sacristy projects, contains a wide pointed window. But the special interest of the place is the pointed barrel vault, enriched with surface ribs and covered with overlapping stone flags, the characteristic finish for small churches from now on.

Before his death in 1400 the same Earl of Douglas expelled a convent of Benedictine nuns from Lincluden in Galloway and started to rebuild the place as a college. And the collegiate church has come down as one of the purest examples of Decorated Gothic in Scotland. As finally completed in the fifteenth century it included an unaisled choir of three bays, with a vaulted crypt below the eastern one, and a nave of four bays with a single aisle to the south, the latter opening into a transeptal chapel at its south-eastern corner. It was probably vaulted throughout. The choir, indeed, seems to have had a pointed barrel vault with surface ribs above its main vault, in which case overlapping flagstones would be the outer covering. Of the whole, the choir is the only part substantially intact. Screened from the remainder by a stone pulpitum, enriched with a sculptured frieze, it is amply lit by large windows, once richly traceried. The piscina and sedilia on one side, and the sacristy door opposite beside the superb tomb of the Princess Margaret, daughter-in-law of the founder, are integral parts of a scholarly and unified design, expressed in the vernacular and remarkable for the vitality of its detail.

A definite contrast to Lincluden is afforded by the contemporary church of the Cistercian abbey at Melrose, the conception not of a single mind but of no fewer than five master-masons, each of whom has impressed his own individuality upon the particular part of the structure for which he was responsible. When this abbey was sacked by the English in 1322, King Robert Bruce granted certain feudal dues, estimated to be worth £2000 sterling, towards the reconstruction. The church was thereupon repaired, only to fall victim to the 'auld enemy' once more. In 1385 Richard II, not content with quartering himself and his troops upon the abbey, fired the place on leaving, so that it was 'clene brent and exiled,' and the church had thereupon to be rebuilt. But the English King, on reflection, must have felt some degree of compunction, since he granted the monks of Melrose remission of certain tolls to help their finances. Funds came in gradually, from King Robert's grant in the first place, then through Papal grants of indulgences, and finally from the acquisition of benefices. And the work of reconstruction seems to have been started before the end of the fourteenth century and to have continued until the first decade of the sixteenth century, when it ceased, while the church was still unfinished, on account of the poverty of the community.

As a nut encloses its kernel, so the last church of the abbey rose round the ruin of its predecessor. Then as each division was finished the old core was pulled down. The plan now provided an unaisled presbytery with side chapels in échelon, transepts with eastern chapels, and a nave with side aisles as well as a chapel aisle on the south side, like Elgin, the cloister precluding a corresponding aisle on the north. Moreover, to avoid interference with the cloister, the side aisle on the north was kept to the same narrow width laid down by the builders of the first church in 1136, the year of the foundation. All divisions of this new church were ribvaulted. The part first built was the presbytery and its chapels. None but a Yorkshire master-mason could have fashioned this superb eastern arm, lofty and sheer, richly arcaded, and amply lit by great windows on all sides, filled with curvilinear and perpendicular tracery, the latter type predominating. His name remains unknown together with that of his successor, who designed the north transept. The south transept, however, that rich translation from northern France, is identified with the name of John Morow 'BORN IN PARYSSE CERTAINLY AND HAD IN KEPYNG AL MASOUN WERK OF SANT ANDROYS, YE HYE KIRK OF GLASGW, MELROS AND PASLAY, OF NYDDISDAYLL AND OF GALWAY.'

Comparisons drawn between the architecture of the east and south gables are as fruitless as they are inevitable. Each is an inspiration; one reflecting the sharp clear air of the Yorkshire Wolds, the other the sun-drenched atmosphere of the Oise. But it may be admitted that the western limb hardly comes up to the standard of the rest—apart from its pier arcade, which has distinct affinities with the choir of Carlisle cathedral, built about a century

65 Aberdeen Cathedral. The crowstep gable of the porch and the
machicolation of the tower are both typical

66 Ladykirk, Berwickshire. The church is of all-stone construction, and was originally built by James IV about 1500

before. The poverty of design and workmanship in the western bays, indeed, implies serious financial stringency. Even so, this was one of the richest fabrics ever built in Scotland. And its ruin is an historic document from which one learns how far the Cistercians had abandoned their first principles. Rich carvings, tabernacled niches, storied glass, and an ornate tower, nothing is wanting from the artistic armoury of the time. Yet in one respect, at least, traditional practice was followed, for the monastic choir remained enclosed within screen-walls of solid stone, in order to preserve some degree of solitude and privacy, now that the place had become a popular pilgrim resort. It was with a view to this traffic that the nave took the shape that it did.

In most Cistercian churches the nave had become superfluous after the Black Death, when the Conversi, to whom the nave was appropriated as their choir, ceased to exist as a class within the community. At Melrose, however, the Conversi seem to have been succeeded by tenants and servants. The nave, at all events, finally came to be used by the parish, either as a privilege or as a right. And this secular use of the nave led later to the construction of a Reformed church within the three eastern bays. To make this, the western crossing arch and the one above the pulpitum were filled in, and the central area was then covered in with a barrel vault, which rested upon piers and arches inserted in front of the pier arcade upon that side. As the new vault was lower than the old high vault, the heads of the clearstorey arcade had to be dropped until they came below the new springing level. Thus altered, and in its present state of ruin, the nave is at first difficult to visualise as a whole.

The church of St. Mary at Haddington, built about the same time as Melrose, and of collegiate status from the second quarter of the sixteenth century, harks back to the vernacular. It comprises an aisled nave and choir, the latter square-ended, and unaisled transepts with a massive crossing tower, once surmounted by an open crown spire, like that at St. Giles'. While the central span of the nave had probably an open timber roof, all else was covered in with rib-vaulting. The bay design is two-storeyed and relatively low. Each bay contains a window filled with rather coarse tracery, most of the windows having a central mullion. But the eastern

I

sides of the transepts are blind, for it was now customary to make provision for high carved reredoses behind the altars, which would have covered any windows on the east side. The west doorway has a central pier, and like many others of its time it is round-arched. Fifteenth-century architecture in Scotland tends to revert to Romanesque forms and ornament.

Like Edinburgh and Haddington, the burghs of Aberdeen, Dundee, Linlithgow, Perth, and Stirling were impelled by civic pride to rebuild their churches on a larger scale in and about the fifteenth century. And all of these rebuilt churches are Scottish in character. The parish church of Aberdeen has been largely rebuilt subsequently, while the cathedral is represented by little more than the massive granite-built nave with its great twin-towered façade which may partly be the work of a family of master-masons who were also engaged at Linlithgow Palace and church. The cathedral, indeed, stands apart from its neighbours in this group as the product of an original mind. In it all detail is subordinated to the elemental forms. The flat oak ceiling with its heraldic decorations, which Bishop Gavin Dunbar paid James Winter, the Angus wright, to construct, is one of the most notable features of a remarkable building. St. John's church at Perth has much in common with St. Mary's, Haddington. St. Michael's at Linlithgow bears a considerable resemblance to the church of Holy Rude at Stirling. Both stand on sloping sites. Each has a west tower, an aisled nave and presbytery with a sanctuary in the form of a pentagonal apse, higher in the one case than in the other. Both churches have transepts, or more strictly, transeptal aisles, which, in the case of Stirling, are very shallow. Stirling was designed to have a central tower over the crossing, but this feature never actually took shape. Its nave is covered with a fine mediaeval open timber roof. The aisles and the sanctuary are vaulted. The presbytery was apparently intended to be vaulted also. At Linlithgow there is no doubt that the major spans were designed to have open timber roofs while the rest was vaulted.

Equally characteristic of the native genius are the smaller churches of the fifteenth century, mostly cruciform and unaisled buildings, usually barrel-vaulted and stone-roofed, and sometimes ending in a pentagonal apse. Of such may be instanced the college kirks of Seton, Dunglass, St. Salvator's at St. Andrews, Dalkeith, Arbuthnott, Crichton, and Corstorphine, as well as the parish churches of Ladykirk and Whitekirk. But the most highly developed of the series is the collegiate church of St. Matthew at Roslin, of which the only part to be completed was the choir, dating from 1457. This was founded by Sir William Sinclair, third Earl of Orkney, son-in-law of the founder of Lincluden. His intention was to build a cruciform church, vaulted throughout, and comprising an aisled choir with a continuous ambulatory and low eastern chapels, unaisled transepts and an unaisled nave, the latter equal in width to the choir plus its aisles, altogether a plan unique in the history of Scottish architecture. If the plan is distinctive, the treatment of the membrane is no less exceptional and indeed suggests that an inspired amateur was the prime mover in the enterprise. Inability to visualise the structure as a whole led to difficulties in construction that an experienced master-mason would have avoided, and yet, as each difficulty arose it was surmounted, generally in an ingenious, if unorthodox, way. These departures from the customary technique would of themselves mark this building from its fellows, but an even more obvious difference is the riot of symbolism, allegory, and carved enrichment with which almost every part is overlaid. In the fundamentals little originality is displayed, however. The fabric, generally, stands in rank with those just mentioned. The arrangement of the choir has been taken bodily from Glasgow. The aisle vaults are of the Burgundian type introduced into Britain by the Cistercians. And even the famous 'Prentice Pillar' has a prototype in France, which that architectural purist, Viollet-le-Duc, once likened to a bunch of sausages.

The salient features of ecclesiastical architecture in Scotland from the late fourteenth century until the Reformation may be set down as follows. The fabrics of the larger churches were lighter, smaller in scale, and less lofty in appearance than their forerunners. The eastern arm was either square-ended or in the form of a pentagonal apse. The use of rib-vaulting was extended, although it was rarely handled with the ease and dexterity displayed in France and in England. At the same time, however, there was a reversion to the use of barrel-vaulting, often enriched with surface ribs and covered with overlapping stone flags. The use of barrel-vaulting made the gable windows specially prominent, for the side windows had to be low, with their heads kept below the springing level, in order to avoid groining. The rejection of groining is clearly illustrated where a transeptal aisle projects from a nave, for the vaults do not interpenetrate. What happens is that a gable is raised upon the arch common to both parts and the aisle vault is abutted upon it, leaving an open space between the outer side of the gable and the main roof. Yet interpenetration was commonly practised upon a small scale in secular work.

Pier arcades of the fifteenth century are low and often top-heavy in appearance. The piers themselves are usually octagonal, although in some cases they are round, as in Romanesque work, and in others they are wrought with clustered columns, frequently bearing fillets. Their bases are bell-shaped and much higher than before. Invariably they follow the contour of the pier members. The capitals are often moulded throughout. But most commonly they are carved with bold foliage, sometimes heavily undercut. And among the foliage little figures and grotesques are often introduced as well as shields, painted or carved with coats of arms. Heraldry was now extensively employed as a decorative motif, and most of the carved work was highly painted or gilt. In churches that were rib-vaulted the windows were shaped like a flat-iron and filled with geometric or flowing tracery. In a few rare instances perpendicular tracery is found. Main doorways were usually round-arched, built in several orders and enriched with square, floral paterae. Many of the smaller doorways have three-sided heads. High, moulded base-courses, eaves-courses enriched with paterae, and tabernacled niches containing effigies of saints were extensively employed to enrich the fabric.

After the Reformation the clergy space and the chapels were cleared of screens and thrown open for congregational worship, the pastor taking his station in the midst of his flock. But many churches were then found to be too large for one minister to preach in comfortably, a circumstance that led to the larger churches being divided by solid stone walls to enable different charges to be accommodated in one building. And among the churches thus affected were those of Edinburgh, Linlithgow, and Stirling. In the seven-

67 Steeple of King's College Chapel, Aberdeen. A typically florid
example of the final Gothic phase in Scotland

68 Burntisland Church, Fife.   The church was started in 1592, and the
tower completed in 1759

69 The Laird's Pew, Abercorn Church, West Lothian.   Designed for
the Hopetoun family by Sir William Bruce

70 Corstorphine Church, Midlothian (fifteenth century)

71 Dairsie Church, Fife (1621)

73 Iona Cathedral: window in south side of Choir

72 Carrington Church, Midlothian (1710)

teenth century, when church extension was once more embarked on, the Gothic tradition died hard, witness the church of Greyfriars in Edinburgh, so named because it stood upon ground once the property of the Franciscans. And the outward forms of Gothic are also manifest in the little parish church of Dairsie, which Arch-

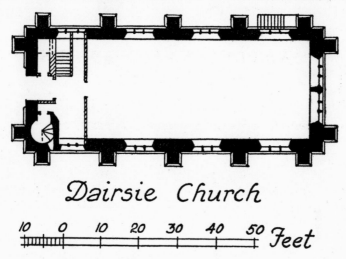

Dairsie Church

10   0   10   20   30   40   50 Feet

bishop Sharp built specially for Episcopalian worship. The last phase of our historic ecclesiastical architecture is well illustrated by the ruined church of Tulliallan, built in 1675, an almost complete parallel to which is the admirable and untouched little church of Carrington, Midlothian, which dates from 1710. The body of this church is oblong and there is a cross-aisle to the north and a bell-tower to the south. Even in so late a building the windows are pointed.

W. Mackay Mackenzie

CASTLES AND TOWERS

THE 'worm-eaten hold of ragged stone,' which in most cases constitutes all that is left of an ancient castle, has a story to tell of a rather more complex and significant kind than is to be gathered from a mere inspection of the ruins. That castles were strong places, were planned and fitted to be defensible and so far were military in character, leaps to the eye. What is not on the face of things so plain is that they were part of a social scheme, that the building of such places in Scotland could be regarded as a matter of 'policy' or good government, being centres of local adminis- tration and normally a check upon lawlessness. They were, in short, the proper homes of a governing class, which had its root in military power and which, relatively few in number, had origin- ally to supplement this weakness with what was hoped to be an impregnable shell of defence, just as the individual member of that class clothed himself on occasion in costly armour. And just as soldiering, in the birth of this class, was its special characteristic and properly confined to it—as the description soldier (*miles*) or knight first indicated a member of it, later a rank, and finally an honour—so the style of residential building favoured by this section of the community reflected its influence and position in the state, and developed in a military Gothic, as churches did in an ecclesiastical Gothic. A castle was as natural a home for a lord of lands as a cathedral a place of worship for a bishop.

Essentially, then, a castle was a fortified dwelling, combining the features of both a residence and a fortification. This type of structure is what distinguishes the period of history it is convenient to call mediaeval, which begins with the breakdown of the Empire of Charlemagne and his immediate successors, the great effort to restore the Roman Empire, with an emperor in the once 'barbarian' land of western Europe not at Rome. But just as that empire had suffered under 'barbarian' incursions on its borders, so its successor, sore harassed by internal division and rivalries, had to meet attacks north, south, and east, by Vikings, Saracens, and Magyars. The machinery of organised central defence broke down. The new imperial power had already weakened. Local magnates tended to settle their differences with the sword, and found themselves forced to undertake by their own hand the protection of their lands and people against private enemies and foreign invaders. They attached dependants by military service and made their homes bases of armed resistance. Thus arose the castle, and out of these conditions came the new bond of social organisation known as the Feudal System.

It was in these circumstances that the first castles began to appear in southern and central France in the course of the tenth century. The new type of edifice came to be known as a *castellum*, from which we get the familiar word. From France proper it was introduced into the young dukedom of Normandy, and with it the feudal network of great landlords as administrative officers attached to the supreme ruler by obligation of military service. The same system, with the castle as its material embodiment, was transferred to England after the Norman conquest, and established there a corresponding form of centralised, efficient, militarised organisation. The Normans were able and systematic administrators, and their business methods, culture, and ecclesiastical orthodoxy appealed to the Scottish kings of the family of Malcolm Canmore and his English queen, Margaret. These kings had a difficult task in welding together and controlling a people of mixed origins and loose adherence. The Norman feudal system seemed to be the sort of thing they required. And so we have, particularly in the reign of

David I (1124-53), the steady introduction of Normans—including men of other stock who had accompanied or followed them—into estates in Scotland to impose the feudal organisation, and such incomers necessarily brought with them the practice of building castles.

These earliest castles were of a primitive type. Not till about the end of the eleventh century did great towers of stone appear even in England, and then at places of special significance, such as London, where the great Tower still survives, and Rochester. Such overpowering erections were as yet neither possible nor called for elsewhere. Least of all could they be expected in Scotland, where existed neither the resources nor the craftsmen. The prevailing example at first, and in Scotland for long after, was a combination of earthworks and timber buildings. A commanding position was isolated by a profound ditch. The preference was for a mount, either adapted from a knoll or ridge or heaped up as a hillock, which, from the French word, was known as a 'motte' or 'mote.' On this was erected the stout timber house of two or three storeys, normally surrounded by a stockade of timber. At a lower level was a curving enclosure with a stockade, which was known as the 'bailey' and which contained subordinate buildings, such as hall, stables, storehouses, and the like. Or the mount might be so extensive as to contain all these on the same site, and the principal building might, in some cases, be not of the nature of a tower, but rather itself a hall of one or at most two storeys, which in time would come to be distinguished as a 'palace.' Thus Rutland Castle in England never had a tower, while an early castle site in Kirkcudbright, a mound of some extent, once surrounded by a loch, is still known alternatively as Castle Fergus or Palace Isle.

The nature of these mote-and-bailey castles can be inferred from contemporary description and the invaluable sewn pictures of the Bayeux Tapestry, which tells the story of the conquest of England. Actual remains, of course, consist only of the earthworks—mound, ditch, and the rampart base of the palisades. These are still to be seen in a remarkable number of cases. Many, partly because they were so originally or have been reduced by weather or other agencies, are of small dimensions, but in other examples the mound, the main element, is of impressive size, like the Bass of Inverurie

74 Doune Castle, Perthshire, erected between 1419-24

75 Hermitage Castle, Roxburghshire.

76 Craigmillar Castle, Midlothian

77 Caerlaverock Castle, Dumfriesshire

by the Don, in Aberdeenshire, that still, after trimming, stands 50 feet high; or is of a plainly artificial and conspicuous character, like the 'Moat' at Hawick, or that of Dalmellington in Lanarkshire. An extensive mound, slightly elevated above its surroundings but differentiated by a yawning ditch, exists near Conon House within sight of that Ross-shire river, and is mapped from tradition as 'David's Castle,' though there is now nothing about it to suggest that description in the later and more familiar sense of the word. A mound of this class is known to have been cleared away near by at Dingwall, where once stood a royal castle. But up and down the country, and particularly in Galloway, such relics are numerous, indicating partly the lines of Norman or Normanised penetration, and partly the way in which their local imitators adopted the new fashion.

Primitive and even cramped as mote-and-bailey quarters must have been, they yet served as the homes of many of the Scottish nobility for a quite considerable time. In England the Mote of Durham as late as 1345 was still crowned with wooden buildings, though the wall round them was of stone. It may be presumed that the houses of the Bruces, that on the Mote of Annan and the other on the great mound at Lochmaben, were of timber. Not till the fifteenth and sixteenth century do we find reason to believe that the term Mote was becoming an anachronism, so that we get the reference to the Mote of Crail in Fife, 'formerly known as the Castle of Crail.'

A special defect of these timber constructions was their liability to be set on fire from outside. In the year 1228 a rising in troublous Moray was marked by the burning of 'wooden fortifications.' As a safeguard against such accidents it became customary to daub the buildings with clay, or even to construct them substantially of such material. Our earliest description of a Scottish tower is in an Arthurian romance, where it is described as a structure of clay. But generally timber, in some such way probably fire-proofed, was the more prevalent substance.

It is true that castles in stone had already, even long before, appeared on Scottish sites, but their spread was slower than we might expect. The necessity or wealth for such expensive construction was not yet within the scope of many. Edinburgh Castle as rapidly reconstructed by the English in 1335-36 had some work in timber, turf, and clay. Yet in East Lothian, about a hundred years before, an imposing and, one might consider, impregnable castle faced with dressed stone had been erected at Dirleton near North Berwick. In its beginning it must have been as much the subject of wondering and awesome comment as the construction of a leviathan liner today. Such erections then seemed beyond the power of merely human skill, so that Yester Castle, of the same century and in the same county, was reputed the work of magic, and its partly underground apartment called the 'Bohall' or 'Goblin's Hall.' Dirleton was to be an active menace to communications and supplies when an English army was hunting for William Wallace and his force in the late summer of 1298. Of the castle of this time there remains still the south-west corner, the large and smaller tower with a rectangular one between them, all handsomely and solidly built in mediaeval ashlar, their 10-foot walls necessary not only for defence but also to carry the stone vaults of chambers in the round towers. The rest of the castle is of probably three different stages at later times, but as a whole it must, from the nature of the site, have been of much the same shape and extent when in the thirteenth century it was constructed for the family of De Vaux.

In this case as in others the layout of the buildings was determined by the advantages of the chosen site. In general, however, the early stone castles followed the model of the mote-and-bailey type. This practice in its simplest form is plainly exhibited in Castle Duffus, some miles north of Elgin. On the mote itself was erected a tower of stone, down from which a stone wall sweeps round to enclose a bailey. Thus we have in more solid material a sheer reproduction of the more primitive earthwork and timber castle, within which the minor buildings would long continue to be of wood.

The same general idea of great tower or dungeon, providing the lordly residence, and attached enclosure, its wall broken by smaller towers to serve as lodgings or other accommodation, in addition to separate structures within or against the wall, can be followed in Bothwell Castle on the Clyde as it existed in the thirteenth century and, in the next, turned out to be a trap for English

78 Castle Kennedy, Galloway

79 Neidpath Castle, above the Tweed at Peebles

refugees from Bannockburn. Led by the Earl of Hereford a large company had reached the castle, expecting protection in a place held for their king. But the politic commander took occasion to

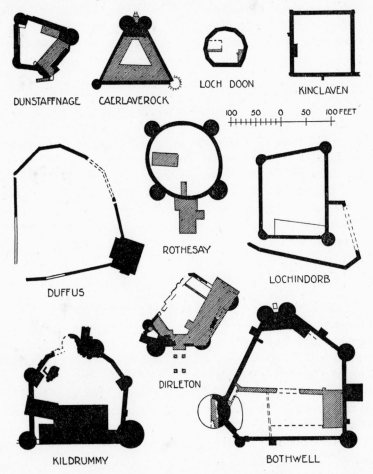

Early Castles. Later Work in Hatching

change sides: men of rank were admitted within the walls but then handed over to the pursuing Scots, who had those left outside at their mercy. The original 'stalwart tower,' as the chronicler called it, is even, in the old fashion, cut off by its own ditch from the courtyard, a feature which we find also in Urquhart Castle on

Loch Ness, which existed at the same early time, but where the present tower is of the early sixteenth century. Like all these thirteenth-century castles, except Dunstaffnage in Argyll, Bothwell suffered extensive demolition at the hands of the Scots in the War of Independence, when it was found that the part played by such places was to serve as bases for the enemy. The 'castle and towers' of Stirling were thus levelled to the ground after Bannockburn; in this usage, as in other such references, the 'castle' means the wall of enclosure. Bruce had swept Edinburgh Rock clear of all buildings that made up the old castle, leaving only the hallowed chapel of St. Margaret. Its new stone erection only began with the raising of David's Tower in the time of his son, and that in the great siege of 1573 was almost obliterated, while much more was sorely damaged, and what we now see is for the most part of later times. Bothwell Castle, as ultimately reconstructed, was reduced to a simple parallelogram of less than half its former dimensions, and the inner semicircle of its partly destroyed great tower closed on the outside with a flat wall. The restoration thus preserved its picturesque outlook over the steep banks of the Clyde, and it must not be assumed that this was a matter of indifference. The people who lived in castles were—as the literature of their time shows— not in the least regardless of natural beauty, the charm of gardens, of flowers, and the song of birds. Many castles besides that of the stage Macbeth had 'a pleasant seat.' On the other hand, a Lord Somerville of a later time could complain of his residence at Cowthally 'that ther was many pleasanter and convenienter stances for a house within the baronie of Carnwath,' but concluded that this site, easily defensible, was originally chosen because of country feuds 'and banding amongst the nobilitie and gentrie, soe that upon the least offence they wer in armes,' when 'the house itself and its situatione was a sure retreat.'

Another survival, the name of which is prominent in the annals of the thirteenth and fourteenth centuries and which suffered similar mishandling, is Caerlaverock, amid marshy terrain some nine miles south of Dumfries. It had its plan fixed, in a very definite sense, by the character of its site, a triangular island in a tiny lake or what was made such by banking, where the castle now shares a reedy quietude with the shy water-hen. A gateway between two towers and a tower at each angle of the side walls with its base make up its triangular outline. Caerlaverock was captured in 1300 by Edward I, a feat glorified in a long contemporary Anglo-French poem but the only fruit of an otherwise barren campaign. The building was, at intervals, twice destroyed by the Scots, and the new erection, which substantially we see, did not reach completion till the middle of the fifteenth century.

The complex character of our earliest castles is thus to be accounted for by two interventions: one, considerable battering and destruction during a prolonged war; the other, the inevitable reconstructions, adaptations, and additions imposed by new needs and mellowing ideas.

All the castles already reviewed show contributions from both causes. The greater part of the front of Dirleton and the whole eastern side had to be restored and new-built in the late fourteenth and throughout the fifteenth century, the eastern corner tower being replaced by the sharp angle of the continuous new building. Bothwell's reduction in size has been noted, and a handsomely windowed hall was adapted to its eastern wall. Caerlaverock was raised again on the determined lines. The Castle of St. Andrews, which had been levelled to the ground, had to be built anew.

In St. Andrews, however, as in the contemporary erection at Tantallon, we see a new conception at work. They occupy roughly similar positions—a coastal plateau with steep rocky faces, two in the former case, three in the other, isolated to landward by a great dry ditch. The main work of each place bestrides the approach, and the great tower is placed centrally in front, the wall-building on either side being retired at an obtuse angle. St. Andrews, however, was first to be amplified with corner towers, like the now fragmentary ones at Tantallon, then in the Reformation War was to have these thrown down, one because within it a cardinal had been slain in the person of David Beaton, after which the place was reconstructed. These castles show the first ostensible departure from the general mote-and-bailey plan: the great tower is not here the crowning feature of the bailey; it is brought to the front of the castle, and through its base goes the entrance reached by the drawbridge. And something more than defensibility comes into the picture. The 'high upreared and abutting front' of Tantallon has surely been designed to impress, to proclaim feudal rank and dominance. More modestly the sixth Earl of Angus in 1528 described it as but such a house as he, like any other man, was entitled to have for protection of himself and his household against their enemies.

Instead of multiplying examples one may dwell upon the castle features now being emphasised in stone construction. In these it is desirable to avoid the fashionable but confusing term 'keep,' which is not mediaeval but a virtually modern imposition. A tower was a tower, great or small, which might indeed also figure as a 'dungeon,' retaining the older word 'donjon' for such an erection. Any other name for it is an affectation. To write, as has been done, of places like walled Dunstaffnage or the compact block of Hermitage in Roxburghshire as 'keeps' is to be mock-heroic.

The defensive positions on a castle or tower were on the wall-head, as is clear from contemporary descriptions and illustrations of sieges. Here, then, was the platform or walk protected to the outside by a parapet, broken by interspaces known as 'crenelles' or 'kernels' and so said to be crenellated. Usually this walk, also known as the 'allure' or the 'alluring,' which in Scots became 'allerine,' was projected upon stone brackets or 'corbels,' the spaces between which, looking to the foot of the wall, were frequently left open, not only offering a means of dropping missiles upon attackers immediately below—particularly those trying to undermine the wall—but also providing drainage from the roof. Such horizontal openings were known as 'machicolations.' Originally a projecting platform of this character was framed upon beams inserted in apertures in the face of the wall, and, being all of timber, was described as 'brattising.' The word was retained for the permanent stone reproduction, in Scots usage becoming 'bartising' and then 'bartisan,' which was a common term for the battlement or 'battling.'

An important fact about this machicolation or bartisan in stone is that it did not become a practice in England—borrowed from France—till towards the close of the fourteenth century. Wherever, therefore, it is found in Scotland, such construction is not earlier than that date, or indeed, as things went, than a good bit after. There is no such crown to the great thirteenth-century tower at

80 Dunnottar Castle, Kincardineshire

81 Tantallon Castle, East Lothian

CASTLES BY THE SEA

82 Kishmull Castle, Barra

Bothwell, but it is massively apparent on the western tower of a later time. Its presence in a building thus becomes an indicator of possible period, even when it is reduced to no more than a projection of this kind above a doorway: not all could indulge in so skilled, and therefore expensive, a work on a big scale.

With this in mind we may look at the simple case of Kishmul Castle on an islet in Castle Bay, Barra, the only impressive structure of the kind in the Outer Isles. Nothing could be simpler than this combination of a great tower and a wall at the water's edge, with houses of a later time along its inner face. The wall-head is broken by only a few gaps as crenellations. The tower is entered at the second floor, to which there had been a built approach, and the stair goes up in the thickness of the wall to the roof, and straight down to the basement. The place looks primitive enough, but a stone machicolation at the wall-head above the door of the tower, and another over the original gate to the court, unmistakably point to the fifteenth century as the earliest date for the building, which is confirmed by its connection with the MacNeils, a family not in possession of the island till shortly after the first quarter of that century.

It is obvious that this machicolation was, to some extent, feudal display. It is continued in positions where it could have no practical value—on the south-east tower of Bothwell over the roof of the chapel, at Caerlaverock above the briefest or no margin of dry land on the outside. Its ornamental aspect as an appropriate architectural finish becomes unmistakable towards the close of the fifteenth and on into the sixteenth century. At Craignethan Castle, picturesquely placed near the Clyde below Lanark, the corbels of the projecting parapet are in two alternating rows, the lower of which blocks any possible apertures above and yet is of no account as a support. The same chequer arrangement, serving only for style, appears in other cases, as at Elcho Castle by the eastern approach to the Carse of Gowrie, Edzell on the North Esk in Angus, and the early sixteenth-century tower of Rusco in the Stewartry. At Stapleton Tower, Dumfriesshire, the late sixteenth-century corbels are but miniatures. What had been in origin a military menace was becoming a show, an imposing cornice. Builders played with it.

In addition to the defence of the wall there was the problem of strengthening the main entrance of the castle, its most vulnerable post. A massive iron-studded door or doors would of course be there, and also a heavy iron-shod timber grating or 'portcullis' that could be speedily dropped from a room above, sliding down in a shallow groove in the stone walls. But, particularly perhaps in face of gunpowder and 'bombards' or heavy guns, more was thought necessary. As at Tantallon, the original spacious arched gateway could be reduced in size. Further, short walls were carried outwards to form a narrow passage of approach, as can be seen in an elaborate fashion at Tantallon, of a simpler character at Dirleton, Kildrummy, and Urquhart. This projecting corridor was the 'barbican.' It needed General Lambert's explosive 'bombshells' in 1650 to blast a way through the barbican at Dirleton. But even before the days of gunpowder great siege-engines throwing missiles of two or three hundred pounds weight could inflict serious damage on a castle, as when in 1304 thirteen of these elaborate wooden contrivances smashed down the upper works of Stirling Castle. On the other hand, all the guns of King James V in 1528 failed to force Tantallon into submission. And that king, when the castle finally came into his temporary possession, made it still more resistant by filling in with masonry the passages and rooms that made great interspaces in its frontal walls. Even guns with their solid shot could be somewhat ineffective against the solid masonry of a castle. In the seventeenth century Caerlaverock, which in 1300 could suffer the siege-engines of Edward I for only a couple of days, held out against the cannon of the Covenanters for over three months.

But the fifteenth century, which was a great building period in Scotland, was to show a much more significant treatment of the castle than these constructive details. In buildings begun towards the close of the preceding century a new formula made its appearance. Hitherto the prevailing idea had been that of a walled enclosure with towers, great and small, and inner buildings for necessary purposes, including probably a great hall. Hall and chambers were the stock subdivisions of domestic edifices. In our usage the former would be 'public room,' the latter those more private or small. In a great tower the main room was the lord's

83   Kildrummie Castle, Donside, Aberdeenshire

84 Castle Campbell, Clackmannanshire, situated between the Burn of Care and the Burn of Sorrow above the town of Dolour (Dollar), and originally known as The Gloume

hall on the first floor. But the size of the household might necessitate another such 'public' apartment on a greater scale, and this would be found within the enclosure. Thus Kildrummy at the time of the siege of 1306 had a 'meikle hall,' which was used in this extremity as a store for corn, part of the victualling of the garrison. Apparently it was of wood, as it was set on fire, and 'The fyre our all the castell spred,' even burning down the gate, so that the other buildings within must also have been of timber. The garrison saved themselves between the double battlements on the wall, but their food supplies had perished and they had to surrender. There was no idea of betaking themselves to a great tower for a 'final stand'; that a place for this was provided in a castle is a piece of modern romanticism.

A free-standing hall would be of two storeys, long rather than high, and hitherto existed as an independent building: in some cases, indeed, as we have seen, it, not a tower, might supply the principal residential quarters, so that a castle could be summarily described as consisting of 'close (*i.e.* enclosure), chawmer, and hall,' as in the Peel of Gargunnock. Duart Castle in Mull is credited with the 'noble addition' of a 'great tower' some time in the first half of the sixteenth century. The 'great tower called the dungeoun' of the 'round castle' at Rothesay was not completed till 1520 and was a new feature. In such places a hall building, which indeed was a type of structure earlier in history than the tower, could be the centre of castle life. Its alternative name, possibly to distinguish it as a separate place from the 'hall' within a tower, was *palatium* or palace. This name, which had no regal significance, was applicable to any such horizontal lodging or similar building, and so could be used for the domestic range of a monastic cloister or for a monastic guest-house, at St. Andrews for example in the fifteenth century, and as to this day the fourteenth-century hospice of the Grey Friars at Inverkeithing is known as 'the Palace,' though until recently it had long provided housing for humble tenants. Some farms, even, still bear this name, presumably because they were once distinguished by a mansion of the palace kind.

It was this more primitive kind of building which was now to assert itself against the prevailing dominance of the tower as the determining factor in the layout of a castle—not universally nor

M

all at once; nor to the complete exclusion of the tower house: that in many cases still best suited the circumstances or means of certain classes of builders. Nor was every one in a position or inclined to pull down a solid existing house in order to replace it with something of a new pattern. Even in the later seventeenth century the first Earl of Strathmore might express his distaste for the old fashion of castles and towers, and yet refrain from laying destructive hands on a house of that sort in which his predecessors had lived, and so would only add to Castle Glamis a second low wing. Similarly, Lord Somerville in 1524 found his house of Cowthally, in the parish of Carnwath, Lanarkshire, to consist of 'three great towers, not one of them joined to other,' and, moreover, planted in no very wholesome surroundings. Still, this 'had been for a long tyme the principal residence of his predecessores.' Therefore his work was to join up these towers by 'quarters' or lines of palace building, forming a court closed on the south by a thick wall. Such building might also, as in this case, be known as a 'gallery,' since, being as a rule about three times as long as its breadth, it could furnish a lengthy apartment of that character, in which it became the practice to hang pictures. The Long Gallery at Dunnottar Palace is a good example.

Only thus could older buildings with their associations be adapted to the new requirements and ideas of living. The most notable example is Linlithgow Palace, which bit by bit was converted from a structure of towers and walls into what we now see as a palace in the full sense of the term, a quadrangle of uniform horizontal building enclosing a court, or, as it was described in the seventeenth century, 'a palace built castlewise.'

But every palace did not reach this consummation, nor was it defective in not doing so. It was the style of the building that warranted the name. The Palace of Fyvie was a comparatively low structure, about 140 feet long, extended from an earlier tower and terminating symmetrically in another tower. Its present handsome façade, however, owes much to embellishment in the early seventeenth century. The Palace of Fetteresso (*Fetterressaeum palatium*) was a similar stretch when in the late sixteenth century it was referred to in these terms: a wing at right angles came later. These are in Aberdeenshire, where the same sixteenth-century

85 Falkland Palace, Fife (sixteenth century)

86 Palace and Church, Linlithgow

88 Vaulted Room, Castle Campbell, Clackmannanshire

87 The Hall, Craigmillar Castle, Midlothian

89 The Hall, Earl's Palace, Orkney

91 Scotstarvit Tower, Fife

90 Borthwick Castle, Midlothian

historian records the presence along the River Deveron 'of many castles and palaces of noblemen.' Fife was another district specially noted for the number of its palaces. A later addition there was the house at Culross still bearing the name of the Palace, though properly that described it more aptly at its earlier stage.

New buildings of course gave full opportunity for the adoption of this palace plan. With others long established, and possibly cramped on site, there had to be adaptation or insertion if more up-to-date provision was to be made. Dirleton offers an example of what could be done in the case of a castle partly destroyed. One whole new side had to be raised on the eastern margin of the rocky shelf. But the builders did not, as might be expected, repeat the earlier design, re-erecting the eastern frontal tower and repeating the smaller one near the far end. Instead, both were reduced to foundations, and the new structure was a long residential block, its outer face substituting for an independent wall. This block presents the normal mediaeval layout. Its ground floor is a vaulted cellarage of cavernous dimensions, since the castle household would be large and the quantity of provisions corresponding, mainly furnished by rents in kind and the produce of the demesne ('mains') or 'mensal' (table) lands. Above the vault is the long hall, a single high storey that had a gabled roof, one end of which communicates with the lord's private apartments, the other with the service offices and the kitchen, the latter in this case being a lofty domed apartment with two yawning hearths, one hatch to the bakehouse or 'pastry' below and another to a well. A castle kitchen is easily identified by its huge fireplace, sometimes big enough to have its own lighting, by one window at Dunnottar Palace, as many as three at Borthwick Tower, but at the original tower of Crichton Castle forming almost the whole of the tiny kitchen.

An effective use of the new conception is seen in Castle Doune, picturesquely placed beside the River Teith, which was being erected towards the close of the fourteenth and in the early fifteenth century. From a tall tower block at one end, providing a private suite in a semicircular turret, runs a façade partly composed by a hall range in two floors half the height of the tower, windowed to the outside and gable-roofed. Round the farther corner there is communication with an oblong kitchen tower. What is this but

the stock mediaeval plan we have already seen on one side of
Dirleton, and which can be followed at St. Andrews, the hall
provision between private residential quarters at one end and

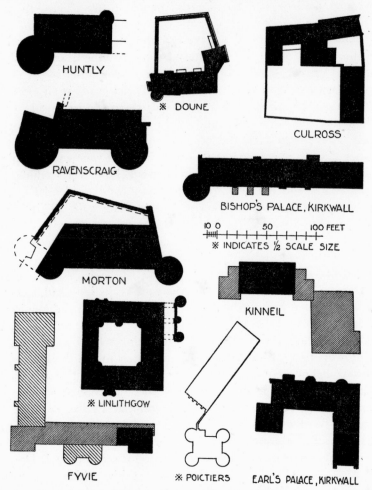

Palace Plans. Later Work in Hatching

kitchen equipment at the other? The entrance to the interior is
a trance through the base of the main tower, and the hall here as well
as the lower range are reached by outside stairs from the courtyard.
Forestairs to the first floor were to be a usual convenience of town

93 Courtyard, Crichton Castle, Midlothian, with its diamond-shaped rustication

92 Courtyard, Caerlaverock Castle, Dumfriesshire Early Renaissance (*c.* 1638)

94   Stirling Castle

houses. At Doune, then, we have not only a more spacious living interior, but also an effective design on the outside.

In other examples a tower continues, but as subordinate to the main palace building, no more the nucleus of structures. A tower had a constructional advantage in the fact that each floor provided a room with an independent entrance from the spiral stair. The 'Palace of Strathbogie,' so called in 1544, when its name was changed to Huntly, is thus equipped at one corner with a round tower; the ornate upper works are of the early seventeenth century. Rait Castle, in Nairnshire, follows the same lines on a smaller scale, a round tower projecting from one angle of a long building.

A number of the new plans based on palace building derived from the prior existence of a free-standing tower with an adjacent bailey or courtyard, the owners of which rose in status and wealth. Craigmillar Castle thus had its beginning, but in the sixteenth and seventeenth centuries the line of the enclosure was transformed into continuous ranges of building. We see the same treatment at Castle Campbell, of old known as 'the Gloume,' picturesquely situated between high moorland and river gorge in the Ochils above Dollar. It exhibits the successive stages—an original motehill, a great tower, and a bailey subsequently converted into lines of residential quarters.

More regular and compact, however, is the development of Crichton Castle on a bare slope overlooking the head-water of the Tyne in Midlothian, the castle which was the 'loved resort' of Sir Walter Scott. In origin a somewhat cramped tower, it expanded with the fortunes of the family into a three-sided enclosure, and then late in the sixteenth century was completed on the remaining side by an edifice with quite unique features, the most striking of which is the inner face rising from a columned portico and coursed in stones hewn in facets 'diamond-pointed.' This was the Italianate design of its then owner, the nephew of Queen Mary's Bothwell and erratic favourite of King James VI. No other similar piece of exotic grandeur is to be seen in the country.

Elsewhere we find the palace building rather a separate erection within the castellated surroundings, as at the castles of Stirling and Edinburgh, though in both cases they crowned in part a section of the higher level of the rock. What the old historian calls 'ane

N

prettie palice in the castell of Stirling' probably owes its sixteenth-century Renaissance details to the direction of French masons, and similar influence has plainly been at work on Falkland Palace, a building wholly of that character, the original tower and its

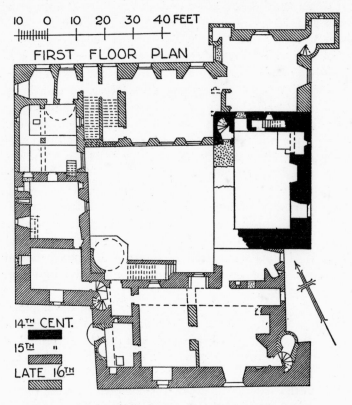

Crichton Castle, Midlothian.   Development from tower

appurtenances, which had stood to the north, having been totally removed.

At Dunnottar Castle the 'Palace' of the Earls Marischal, a three-sided structure, is also disposed as to the main part on the brink of the rock, but wholly detached from the other buildings on that ample, almost insulated plateau 'swilled with the wild and wasteful ocean,' where the cliffs for the most part do the office of a wall. It is far from the old fourteenth-century tower and but one of several

95 The Palace, Stirling Castle. The old style and the new mingle in the early sixteenth-century palace

96 Smailholm Tower, Roxburghshire

scattered buildings of different dates. Dunnottar of itself exhibits the main successive stages in castle architecture.

So prevalent was the use of the term 'palace' in Scotland for this type of hall-building in country and town, as common as *palazzo* in Italy of like origin, that eighteenth-century visitors could record it frequently, and one at least put it down to Scottish ostentation. But the term in the sense used is known also in England and Wales, though it stuck more closely in Scottish nomenclature, and in contrast to the earlier manner of building enables us to distinguish the later or modified castles as constructed on the palace plan.

It was a material embodiment of the desire for freer and more pleasant homes. It exhibits the gradual divergence from military standards and necessities of life. People then had much the same fundamental desires as we have today. Personal security we have learned to achieve by other means. Furnishings in a castle gave a different feeling to what we see only for the most part as bare cold walls. Coloured hangings on the room, rushes or aromatic herbs on the floors, cushioned settles and carved or metal-bound chests, heavily draped beds, food and drink in plenty—these were the precursors of our more voluptuous equipment, but they were the best possible in their time, even as the gardens, though limited and simple in their plants and trees, gave them, too, all the pleasure to be derived from these amenities. There was less violence in the history of most castles than their appearance suggests; in the late fifteenth century the Earl of Angus could let his castle of Bothwell on lease to a tenant, be himself refused admission by his tenant, and take his case for judgment before the Lords of Council, who held the lease to be, on that account, terminated.

One element of a baronial castle must not be overlooked, as it marks a service in one important direction, that of local administration. The holder of lands as a barony was empowered to exercise justice for all within its bounds as far as the extreme measure of 'pit and gallows.' The pit was the prison, and in many castles and towers such a cell, often possible for but a single occupant, can be identified. There is on record the case of a man forcibly confined in 'the pit of Tulliallan' in Fife, 'where through want of entertainment (*i.e.* food) he famished and died of hunger.' Such a

place was normally made accessible only from above and was thus
really a sort of pit, as can be seen at Dunvegan Castle in Skye,
though at Tantallon the place is more roomy and is reached by a
door, which opens upon a sheer drop.   The most weird example

'Pits,' *i.e.* Prisons in Castles
At Dirleton: Upper and Lower Prisons

is the 'bottle dungeon' at the Castle of St. Andrews, where it is
hewn out in that shape to the depth of 25 feet in the solid rock
below the Sea Tower.   Little better is the partially rock-walled pit
reached by a hatch in a corner of Dirleton Castle.   A castle was
not only a residence and a fortalice but also a seat of territorial
justice.

Hitherto we have moved among the greater and more complex

castellated constructions, which further display modifications and additions at different grades of social life extending over many centuries. At Dirleton a handsome house of the new Renaissance type, with crowstepped gables, that might have stood in the street of a town, was erected behind the ancient thirteenth-century corner. An even more ornate building of the same class, with carved pediments over the windows, was built early in the seventeenth century against the inside of the east wall of Caerlaverock, facing a fifteenth-century house on the opposite side, and its large outer windows pierced the embattled wall above and below. Such was the sewing of cloth upon an old garment, and such provision made some of these ancient holds inhabitable for at least a century longer.

But ranking below these greater edifices we have a whole range of castellated or typically defensive houses corresponding to different classes of owners, from the lord of many acres to one of no more than would now be reckoned a farm of moderate size. From these minor ranks come the many towers of varying dimensions that, here and there all over the country, bear witness to a life and order that have passed away. In a region liable to foray and feud a place of refuge was a necessity, and nothing was so well suited to this need as a tower of mortared stone, which externally at least could not be set on fire, and which offered a narrow front of defence for a small number. A tower was the characteristic dwelling of a Scottish laird. Dumbiedikes in *The Heart of Midlothian* was such a dwelling, a tower that was a 'single' house, that is, had but one room on each floor reached by a narrow turnpike stair in 'a half-circular turret' crowned with a 'bartisan' or battlement. It was in law a fortalice or 'tour of (de)fens.' And Scotland bristled with these mansions of much subdivided lordships.

Within a restricted space of this kind rose the usual mediaeval provision—the lord's hall, his lady's bower, chamber and kitchen and store, the last usually a vaulted apartment as ground floor. A big tower, indeed, might be built as one high vault upon another, these again being divided by wooden floors. On the other hand, 'The Threave' (as it was styled), a Douglas tower on an island in the Kirkcudbright Dee, though in existence before 1400 and so one of the earliest, has, like so many Border towers, but one as a basement. It was the floors, laid in single planks upon the beams, with the couples of the roof, that are in question when we read of a stone tower being burned.

Access to the floors was provided, almost as a rule, though there are exceptions, by a spiral stair of stone which, until late in castle history, was always treated merely as a convenience, not as a subject for dignifying ornament. Room for it might be found in the thickness of the wall—and mediaeval builders favoured thick walls, which indeed were imperative where a stone vault had to be sustained—or in a rounded projection inside or a turret outside, which again might rise only from the first floor, at which level too might be the main entrance, the basement having its own door or being reached by a stair down from the interior, or both ways. A stair continuous from the ground entrance to the roof is rather an advanced than an early occurrence, though it may be found in the presumably late fourteenth-century tower at Dunnottar. But means of access up and down vary considerably. When the entrance to the tower, as in many examples—at Lochleven, or Pitcruivie in Fife, or Coxton near Elgin, or Lochwood in Dumfriesshire—was at first-floor level, the approach to it was by an outside stair, stone-built or, in some cases, of timber. This floor was the main one, the hall, and the stair to the upper parts commonly opened at the far end. But all these arrangements were liable to vary according to convenience or necessity.

Almost invariably grouped with the tower were various humble outhouses; the indispensable stables of a people who travelled beyond their homes on horseback, the byre of a largely pastoral community, and it might well be a barn and a brew-house. How many such annexes there might be depended on the resources of the householder. They particularly were the subjects of looting by an aggressive neighbour or a foreign foray. Some protection was provided in an enclosing wall, not so high or formidable as the 'curtain' of a castle proper, which was known as a 'barmkin' or 'barnekin.'

A notable defensive feature of the towers was the iron 'yett' or gate behind the stout wooden door, which for all its thickness might be burned through. The 'yett' was, like the portcullis, a grating, but hung on hinges, not dropped, and was composed of iron bars alternately penetrating and clasping each other in a fashion

97 Rowallan Castle, Ayrshire. Dating from 1560

99 Kilcoy Castle, Black Isle

98 Dalhousie Castle, Midlothian, showing grooves for gaffs
of drawbridge

peculiar to Scotland. In 1606 the Privy Council was ordering that, save in the houses of responsible barons, these gates should be turned into plough-irons or other useful implements. Nevertheless a few still survive, as at Comlongon Tower in Dumfriesshire and Coxton in Moray.

It has been the custom to speak of the smaller towers as 'peels,' an unnecessary and, in this case, misleading term like 'keep.' A peel was an enclosure, in origin and generally of timber, a stockade, which is frequently recorded as being burned. It might surround a house with its byre and stables. Thus in the ballad of *Jamie Telfer* we read how when the raiders from Bewcastle across the Border

> Cam to the fair Dodhead,
> Right hastily they clam the peel;
> They loosed the kye out, ane and a',
> And ranshackled the house right weel.

A picture of a Border foray in four lines. A 'peel-house' was therefore a house within a peel, and a 'peel-tower,' if the expression can be found, a tower similarly placed.

For households of any size or importance a tower, unless on an inconveniently large scale, offered rather limited accommodation. There were methods of amplifying this. One was the hollowing out of smaller, often tiny, chambers or closets in the thickness of the walls. One such can be seen off the first floor in the late fourteenth-century (possibly later) tower at Dunnottar, no more than a cubicle. They are common in the bulky, low-roofed towers of the century after. At Comlongon, which rises to 65 feet aboveground, one wall, increased to $13\frac{1}{2}$ feet in thickness, while the others are 10 feet, is used for this provision. The most striking case, however, is Elphinstone in East Lothian, of the same century, where the 8-foot walls are honeycombed with many small chambers, and stairs are provided for their convenience.

It was probably easier to secure fuller accommodation by adding a short wing to the main building, if not indeed what amounted to another tower, as was the case at Clackmannan. At Ruthven Castle, three miles from Perth, we do have two independent towers of successive dates, later joined up by an intermediate building. We have seen how at Cowthally there were three such separate towers. But the 'tower with a jamb,' *i.e.* wing (Fr. *jambe*), was the ordinary resource. We may set aside the idea that such an extension was provided as a flanking defence. The place most in need of protection was the entrance, but in very many cases the wing occurs on a different side. In others it does overlook the door, and in the latter examples may be provided with a gun-hole opening in that direction. But the general idea, covering all varieties, is that of accommodation. In the wing, too, the rooms being smaller have ceilings lower in proportion, and there are thus more apartments in its height than in the main block. At Preston Tower beside Prestonpans there are six storeys in the tower proper, but seven in the wing.

What really was behind this tower plan can be seen very clearly in Borthwick Castle, Midlothian, conspicuously placed above the valley of the Gore Water, where it occupies the site of what had been a mote-and-bailey castle. It is certainly a most favourable testimony to fifteenth-century planning and construction. Here we have an unusual example of two wings attached to one side of the main block. In its height of just over 78 feet to the machicolated parapet, this noble building contains 30,000 tons of masonry, of which not less than 12,000 tons are of ashlar, as then known, carefully squared and dressed stones forming the wall-face as well inside as out. Its doorways show both the wide fifteenth-century chamfer or bevel and the edge roll.

We observed at Dirleton the characteristic mediaeval arrangement of the east side—the long central hall with the family suite at one end and the kitchen offices at the other. If now, instead of continuing the lordly and servile departments in the line of the great public room, we turn them at right angles, preserving their relative positions, we get the plan of Borthwick. The vaulted stores are in the basement, with an independent entrance as well as access from the interior; the main door opens on the first-floor lofty, vaulted hall, above which another vault supporting the roof has been subdivided horizontally, and each section of the house has its own stair. Borthwick Castle has been, with some intervals, in regular occupation down to the present day. Time may antiquate but cannot of itself destroy this dignified monument of the remote past. Furnishing and some minor and external details apart, it is

100 Fordyce, Banffshire

101 Craigcaffie, Galloway

103 Yett, Greenknowe Castle, Berwickshire

102 Detail of Corbelling, Fordyce, Banff

substantially as it was when, on a June night, Mary Queen of Scots slipped out in male attire to join Bothwell and accompany him to Dunbar. And then it was nearly a century and a half old.

But towers, like the castles of larger scale, underwent, during the fifteenth and into the next century, changes that for many amounted to transformation. They can be grouped only in classes, not in a series. The parapet retires, is reduced in extent, is confined to one side, or even, as at Coxton, to a corner, finally disappears. The corbel course or brackets on which it projected becomes a continuous cornice or, in examples in north-eastern districts, a rather fantastic key pattern. There is more individual treatment at work. With the diminishing or disappearance of the parapet comes the gabled instead of the flat roof. Even Hollows (*i.e.* Holehouse) Tower, beautifully situated on the Esk below Langholm, on the margin of the old Debatable Land, a sixteenth-century substitute for an earlier erection, shows a much restricted parapet on most ornate corbelling, a gabled roof, and a chimney-head at one end confronted with a sort of claw-shaped bracket at the other, the purpose of which—observation or a beacon—is not certain.

There is, too, a marked change in plan, influenced, as in the greater mansions, by the palace model. We hear not of the tower with an adjacent or detached hall but of the 'great house with a tower.' And the tower is as likely to be round as oblong, and to be matched with another, the pair at opposite corners of one long side or diagonally, as was the preferred fashion beyond the Forth. Here again the service of flanking is introduced as an explanation, though defensive elements are really weakening, and the factor at work is apparently the desire not to block or diminish lighting, so that, as at Dundas in West Lothian and Pitcullo in Fife, the additional later tower is awkwardly and unsymmetrically placed for no other possible reason.

It might be desired, also, to retain an earlier tower in use and combine it with a new 'great house.' How this could be done we can see at Kilravock, Nairnshire, where the 'mekle tour' of old was linked to the later building by an intermediary tower carrying up a stair which served both portions, a scale-stair, too, of the type now spreading in use, with straight flights and landings.

Indeed, Scottish lairds were loath to dispense with their tower type of house. For one thing, it was no light matter to dispose of a substantial building, however inconvenient. As we have seen, additional accommodation might be provided adjoining but independent of the time-honoured tower. But something might also be done with the original building itself. This is how Spedlins Tower in Dumfriesshire was adapted. The two topmost floors have walls only 4 feet thick, while the walls below are of 10 feet. But the floors specified have been reconstructed to suit seventeenth-century requirements, having rooms opening on each side of a central corridor, with a twin roof atop. At least more divided accommodation, and so more privacy, could thus be secured. The roof as the 'fighting-top' of the tower was no longer a matter for consideration.

It was the upper parts of such a building that were the pleasantest, and where the tower came to be restricted in dimensions we get efforts to take advantage of this characteristic by making the uppermost floor oversail those below, and, where the tower is round, carrying it out on the square. There are several examples of this device dating from the second half of the sixteenth century, one being at Claypotts, near Broughty Ferry, for a time the property and home of John Graham of Claverhouse, Viscount Dundee. The round towers at diagonal corners of the mansions are both expanded in this way, as if a single-storeyed house had been planted on the top of each.

There are other cases in which a two-storeyed domestic building has actually been erected within the parapet of the pre-existing tower, as was done in the first quarter of the seventeenth century at Preston, Midlothian, and at Niddrie-Seton in West Lothian. We may take as the first step in this odd contrivance the late roofing-in of some part of the parapet walk, as we see done at Comlongon Tower, Dumfriesshire, and Ruthven Castle, near Perth.

And yet even in that time of wholly new ideas in house-building, towers could still be raised, though with more thought of convenience and appearance than of mere solid strength. Amisfield Tower, Dumfriesshire, is a notable example, dated 1600, the uppermost part of which has its lines broken by two-storeyed turrets, round and rectangular, some with their tiny roofs rising even above

104 Claypotts Castle, Angus. Built between 1569 and 1588

105 Pinkie House, Midlothian. Built by Chancellor Seton in 1613

107 Craigievar, Aberdeenshire

106 Midmar, Aberdeenshire

108 Barcaldine Castle, Argyll

109 Doocot, Dunure Castle, Ayrshire

110 Doocot, Tantallon, East Lothian

MEDIAEVAL DOOCOTS

the lofty gabled main roof. The body of the building is of rubble, but these upper expansions are faced with ashlar, and the plain suggestion is that the rubble walls were once harled, so as to throw the ashlar work into relief. How effective this can be, may be seen at Coxton Tower in its present state, where against the lime-washed

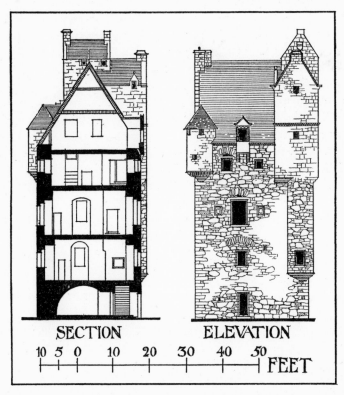

Amisfield Tower, 1600, Dumfriesshire

harling the ashlar of the roof turrets and corner parapet gets its decorative value. Scotstarvit in Fife, however, of about the same time, is wholly ashlar-built, and even preserves the now old-fashioned parapet round its gabled roof.

With buildings of greater bulk the equipment of the upper storeys with turrets of different shapes and dimensions, containing the sort of small room known as a 'study,' provided a picturesque class of architecture which has been styled 'Scottish baronial.' It is well represented in the earlier block of Castle Fraser, Aberdeenshire, in Castle Stewart, some miles out of Inverness on the way to Fort George, and Kilcoy Castle, a Mackenzie house again occupied, in the Black Isle. Such mansions are among the last representatives of a true national style.

With them the long record of castle building makes a handsome end. By the middle of the seventeenth century the practice was a thing of the past. Moralising upon it in his own case, the first Earl of Strathmore (1677), with his own Castle Lyon, now Huntly, and Glamis in his mind, could comment that 'such houses truly are worn quyt out of fashione, as feuds are . . . the country being generally more civilised then it was of ancient times.' It was no longer necessary for a man to 'make himselfe a prisoner' in such a place. 'There is no man,' he continues, 'more against these [*sic*] old fashion of tours and castles then I am.' The castle and 'tower of fens' had become as obsolete as a suit of armour.

117 Clackmannan Tower, showing cap-house and defensive machicolation

116 Affleck Castle, Angus

118 The Study, Culross, Fife

Ian G. Lindsay

<hr>

THE
SCOTTISH BURGH

<hr>

'THERE's the kingdom o' Fife, frae Culross to the East Nuik, it's just like a great combined city—Sae mony royal boroughs yoked on end to end, like rapes of ingans, with their hie-streets, and their booths, nae doubt, and their kraemes, and houses of stane and lime and forestairs—Kirkcaldy, the sell o't, is langer than ony town in England.' So remarks Andrew Fairservice in one of his orations to Frank Osbaldistone. He picked, needless to say, the most thickly populated part of Scotland, but nevertheless it reminds us that the country did not consist, even two or three hundred years ago, of nothing but treeless wastes and endless tracts of moor inhabited only by crofters. The Highlands, it is true, are not remarkable for towns—in fact, there are hardly any which are not modern—but the Lowlands, and more especially the east coast, are dotted with numerous burghs many of which still contain picturesque old houses clustered in strange crooked ways or standing by the old harbours which were once busy trading-centres with the Baltic and the Low Countries. Such places are largely the production of the seventeenth and eighteenth centuries; before that time trade was comparatively small, and the larger towns which rose previous to the Reformation grew for other causes. Briefly, these causes were the Church and the Court. Several places owe their origin to great ecclesiastical foundations and, as in the cases of

P   77

St. Andrews, Glasgow, and Aberdeen, were further enriched by the presence of Universities. The King of Scots had palaces in places other than his capital of Edinburgh, and we may take it that Linlithgow, Stirling, and Dunfermline became towns of reasonable standing because of the periodical visits of the Stewarts.

Though, of course, the layout of all these towns, apart from the natural surface of the ground, is governed by different factors, one clustered round a harbour, another growing from beneath the walls of a castle or standing near a great church, yet the general plan has much in common, and a knowledge of this plan is a help to the better understanding of the various buildings contained in the burgh. The main hub of life was the High Street and the main thoroughfare was known as such, almost without exception. It is generally of fair width, and along it stand the finest buildings, the town houses of the neighbouring lairds, the mansions of the richer merchants, and the Tolbooth or Town House. The width and central position of the High Street has often resulted, however, in the destruction of its older houses, for it has generally remained the centre of business, and hence if the town prospered the old houses have been pulled down to make way for banks and shops, so that the High Streets of Dunfermline, Ayr, Alloa, Lanark, and other places hardly retain a building more than a hundred years old.

In this connection it may be noted that before the eighteenth century, and only to a limited extent even then, the shop as we know it hardly existed. Down narrow closes the craftsman was to be found in his workshop, while the ordinary commodities of life were sold in the markets; hence the number of fairs which were held, the booths mentioned by Andrew Fairservice, and the pedlars who plied their trade in town and country. These fairs and markets were generally held in the High Street, though there are some towns with places set apart. The spacious Marketgate of Crail is a good example; in Edinburgh are the Grassmarket and Lawnmarket; while in Kelso as well as a great Market Square are Wood, Coal, and Horse Markets.

The tolbooth already mentioned as an ornament of the High Street is, if it has been left alone, one of the most picturesque features of our towns. It is fortunate that a number still remain, but many have been demolished, some owing to supposed or real lack of accommodation, and others, doubtless, due to their 'island' sites. The tolbooth of Edinburgh, or 'Heart of Midlothian,' which stood near the west front of St. Giles' Church, and that of Elgin which stood in the centre of the High Street, also to the west of its parish church of St. Giles', both vanished over a hundred years ago. In 1819, two years after that of Edinburgh, the splendid tolbooth of Leith followed, in spite of the protests of Sir Walter Scott. These, unfortunately, are only a small minority of those which suffered a like fate.

The origin of the word tolbooth is quite literal, for it was the booth at which the tolls or taxes were collected. In later years the term was applied more freely, and the building known as the tolbooth was really the town hall; in it on the first floor was the Council Chamber and the local Court-room, while below were the cells, whose chief occupants were generally debtors.

The earlier tolbooths were built as towers serving as a municipal place of strength, but by the end of the sixteenth century the tower became an ornamental part of the building rather than the whole, and its chief function apart from marking a place of such importance was to house the town bell. As a symbol of authority the municipal tower still exists. In the late eighteenth century it developed into a classical spire such as or perhaps more imposing than was usual in the churches of the period, while by the late nineteenth century we find an elaborate tower as part of the Glasgow City Chambers. It is the same in other countries; at Vadstena in Sweden is a little town hall with a thick-set tower which would not be out of place in a Fife burgh, while the chief feature of the great town hall of Stockholm finished in 1923 is its high tower with its bells and the three golden crowns of Sweden gleaming at the top. In Scotland the earlier of the remaining tolbooths date from the end of the sixteenth century, and for long they were influenced by the Low Countries, but it was only an influence of general form. There is not, and never was, anything to compete with the Raadhaus of Brussels or of Oudenaarde, but the quaintly shaped steeples of Musselburgh and South Queensferry have affinities to the simpler forms of the Netherlands. Though altered and added to, the tolbooth at Tain in Ross-shire is a good illustration of the transition between a regular tower of defence and a tower ornamental. It is sturdy in outline, and from each angle is corbelled a turret with a conical stone roof, while in the centre arises another and larger cone of stone, within which is a Dutch bell dated 1616. The Canongate tolbooth is also early, bearing the date 1591. Its tower is pierced by a pend, but small turrets project at the top and the whole is crowned by a slated spire. The Council Chamber, of slightly later date, is built alongside, and being, as usual, on the first floor, is reached by an outside stair. In Musselburgh the tolbooth, which was probably built about the same time, has also a pend under the tower, and the block containing the Council Chamber which is attached at one side still retains a parapet walk supported by corbels. It has been enlarged later, and a new Council Chamber was built behind in the classic style of 1762. Soon after this all military survivals died out, and the tolbooth at Dunbar, which was built about 1620, has, except for its tower, a purely domestic aspect with crowstepped gables and dormer windows. The tower, which is hexagonal and upon whose walls are a couple of sundials, is capped by a spire, and though the building is small, it remains the most attractive feature of the High Street. Though its tower dates from 1783, the main block of Culross tolbooth was built at this period; Dysart is a little earlier, but the upper part of the tower is likewise eighteenth century. Other seventeenth-century tolbooths are to be found in Kirkcudbright, a very good example; Hamilton, which is somewhat altered; Glasgow, of which only a tower remains isolated in the traffic; Clackmannan, which too is represented by only the tower; and Dingwall, which has been so mutilated by alterations that it is not very interesting. The Midsteeple or town hall of Dumfries, built in the first decade of the eighteenth century, carries on the tradition, for its tower and spire are typically Scottish, somewhat resembling those at Stirling and Linlithgow. Of these two, the latter was rebuilt in 1848 after a fire, and though part of the old work remains, the termination of the tower was not replaced. At South Queensferry the tower was remodelled about 1720, but, though it is still attractive, the outline of the slated spire is not improved by a rather clumsy clock erected during the last century. At Strathmiglo and Auchtermuchty in Fife are eighteenth-century towers of a type peculiar to that county. They are terminated by

119 Lerwick Tolbooth, Shetland

120 Tolbooth and Mercat Cross, Inverkeithing, Fife

122 Kirkcudbright Tolbooth, Galloway

121 Stirling Tolbooth

short spires, and the balustraded parapets are similar, though later in date, to those on the churches of Anstruther Easter, Pittenweem, and Cupar. Built into the tolbooth at Strathmiglo, which now is a recreation room, is a panel which has carved upon it a coat of arms and the date 1734. At Auchtermuchty the tolbooth, which is dated 1728, is still used for its original purpose, but the main block has been spoiled by ungainly modern windows. In Crail the town house has a thick-set tower with a charming pagoda-like roof dating from the eighteenth century, but the base is much earlier, probably sixteenth-century, and the addition is as late as 1814. Though a composite structure, it is very typical and one of the few which still remains standing alone in the centre of the street. It would seem, too, to exert a good influence, for the Council of Crail is one of the few in Scotland which really appreciate the old houses in the town and regard them, if suitably reconditioned, as an asset.

By the middle of the eighteenth century the tolbooth became far more conventional and the quaintly capped steeples gave way to a formal spire such as may be seen in Banff. The town house of Montrose with its arcaded ground floor dates from this period, and Boswell wrote in 1773 that there is a 'good dancing-room and other rooms for tea drinking.' One of the finest of the later town halls was that at Dundee, demolished in 1931, in spite of the strongest protests, in order, it appears, to give a better view of some very dull modern municipal buildings. The Dundee tolbooth was designed by William Adam and finished about 1735. With such buildings as the spired town house of Falkland (1805) the tradition carried on into the nineteenth century.

Among the things kept in the tolbooth were the standard weights and measures. In fact, Pennant notes of Stirling in 1772 that 'The great street is very broad; in it is the tolbooth, where is kept the standard for the wet measures of Scotland.' The Tron or public beam for weighing merchandise often stood by the tolbooths, though in Edinburgh it was some way down the street, near the church which came to be called after it. At Ceres in Fife is a simple little seventeenth-century weigh-house in whose wall is set a stone with a pair of scales carved upon it; on one side is a bale and on the other a weight, while to keep things straight, as it were, is added the motto, 'GOD BLESS THE JUST.' But as a second and more material warning against short measures the jougs hung just below. Jougs are to be found in various parts of Scotland—often hanging to this day in some public place. They consist of an iron collar which was padlocked round the neck of the unfortunate offender and fastened by a strong chain to the tolbooth, or often to the churchyard wall. At least one remains in the latter position within the bounds of Edinburgh at Duddingston.

A close neighbour to the tolbooth was the mercat cross, a symbol whose origin is buried in the mists of antiquity but whose later office was important as the centre from which proclamations were made, where criminals were punished, and to which goods were brought to be sold. The most spectacular crosses were generally confined to the larger burghs, but of these only one remains in its original condition. It, strangely enough, has been deserted by its town and now stands on a waste piece of ground at Preston in East Lothian. These crosses were raised upon a platform surrounded by a parapet to which access was obtained by an internal stair. The base was sometimes circular, as at Preston, but was varied from octagonal, as at Edinburgh, to square. In the centre of the platform stands the cross shaft, upon whose capital often stood a unicorn holding a shield. The seventeenth-century Preston cross is a very charming composition. The lower part or drum is divided by pilasters into eight divisions which, except for two occupied by doors, are filled with semicircular niches with shell-heads. The shaft takes the form of a thin Doric column and is crowned with the usual unicorn. Above each pilaster are sockets for flag-staffs, so that ceremonies must have been gay affairs.

The Cross of Edinburgh, quite the most famous of them all, is, except for the shaft, entirely modern. The old cross was demolished in 1756 and the shaft taken as an ornament to Lord Somerville's grounds at Drum, where it remained for 113 years. In 1869 it was returned to near its old site and was set up within the railings of St. Giles' Church, where it remained till 1885. In that year it was once more placed upon a spacious platform presented to the city by William Ewart Gladstone, and since then proclamations have been read from it as of old by the Lord Provost surrounded by his halberdiers to the citizens of Edinburgh, and by the Lyon King of Arms with his glittering court of heralds and pursuivants

124 Mercat Cross, Preston, East Lothian

123 Mercat Cross, Kincardine-on-Forth, Fife

125 Gifford, East Lothian

to the realm of Scotland. The history of the Cross of Edinburgh is almost that of Scotland, and to retell the national events which have taken place within its shadow would require a large volume.

Another fine cross of the type is at Aberdeen. It was built in 1685 by a mason from Old Rayne for the modest sum of £100, which was paid out of the guild wine funds. It was, however, removed to another site in 1837 and seems to have suffered somewhat, for there is now no stair to the platform and the lower part is open. The parapet is divided into panels in which are circular medallions containing the Royal arms and those of the town of Aberdeen, while on the others are the carved heads of Kings James I-VII, Mary Queen of Scots, and Charles I and II. The shaft, as at Edinburgh and Preston, is terminated by that very favourite Scottish device, the unicorn holding a shield charged with the Royal arms. There are several other crosses of this type in the country, but they are entirely modern, often, however, designed from old pictures or documentary evidence. Such may be seen in Perth, Selkirk, and the Muckle Cross of Elgin.

The more usual type is a shaft set upon several steps of circular or octagonal plan. The term of cross is somewhat misleading, for the cross ecclesiastical is very rare. Banff is, in fact, the only example where the Crucifixion with attendant figures is carved at the head. It now stands outside the town hall, but was at one time, like the shaft of Edinburgh, moved into the country. The story is that the finances of the burgh were very low and the Earl of Fife offered a barrel of sovereigns for the cross. This was gladly accepted, but when the barrel was delivered it was remarkably small. However, in spite of that, the cross left the burgh for some time. Another very interesting example is that of Kilwinning, whose shaft is capped by an ancient cross of wood, the only one in the country. At Inverkeithing the cross dates from the sixteenth century. It was moved from the High Street in 1797 and now stands outside the tolbooth. The shaft is raised on steps, and on two sides of the capital are carved the Royal arms, on the third a Douglas coat, and on the fourth that of Robert III and his queen Annabella Drummond, who frequently resided in the burgh. The unicorn on the top was added in 1688. The majority of crosses still existing date, however, from the seventeenth century, but since they generally stood in the centre of the street, a considerable number have been moved. Often the shaft alone is retained and is either clamped to, or stands near, the walls of the town hall, a position in which it loses all its dignity, as may be seen at Dunbar, Cellardyke, Dunfermline (dated 1695), Alloa, or as at Kirkcudbright where the cross shaft (dated 1610) stands on the tolbooth forestair.

However, there are numbers of fine crosses still standing upon their steps, and they are often to be found in quite small places. One of the most typical is that of Airth, which is dated 1697 and whose octagonal shaft rises from five steps of like plan. The top is ornamented by two sundials and the Elphinstone arms with the motto 'DOE WELL LET THEM SAY.' Across the river from Airth at Kincardine-on-Forth stands another fine seventeenth-century cross rising from six octagonal steps and bearing the arms of the Earl of Kincardine at the top. Such arms were a very favourite ornament; the Bruce arms can be seen at Clackmannan, Mar and Kellie at Alloa, and Moray and Argyll at Doune, though, as at Cockburnspath, formal thistle or other designs were also used. As on the houses of the time, sundials too were frequent. At Lochmaben there is a dial on each face of the top block, and these persisted long after clocks and watches became comparatively common. The crosses of Wigtown, 1748, and Swinton, 1769, still retain them. In fact, the eighteenth-century cross was very like the seventeenth, though the shaft tended to become more classical and instead of a plain square or octagonal pillar developed into a Doric column. The favourite unicorn, too, was not quite as usual, and in some cases the shaft was surmounted by an urn or, as at Galashiels (1695), by a weather-vane of pierced metal. At Campbeltown and Inveraray mediaeval Celtic crosses are set up as mercat crosses, but this, needless to say, was not their original purpose. In recent years several crosses have been erected or restored, some have old shafts, some old steps, as Culross, and some do not contain an old stone of any kind. However, whether old or new, the mercat cross is always an ornament to a burgh and a most fitting symbol of municipal independence.

The providing of water for these communities was a task of

some difficulty. The larger houses were often provided with private wells either in their cellars or gardens, but for the poorer people the public springs and pumps were the only source. Edinburgh first had a system with pipes which brought water from Comiston, a distance of two and a half miles, in 1681. A reservoir or cistern of lead (43×28×6) was built on the north side of the Castlehill, and from it pipes supplied the various 'wells' built down the Royal Mile, several of which remain. Linlithgow has also several old wells, which retain picturesque names, as the Lion Well, Dog Well, and St. Michael's Well, each standing before a wynd named after it. St. Michael's Well is interesting in some ways. It is a simple square structure, but on the top stands a winged angel holding a shield on which is carved the burgh arms, while below is '1720 SAINT MICHAEL IS KIND TO STRAINGERS,' a most unusual inscription for the Presbyterian Scotland of the early eighteenth century. The wells noted above are, incidentally, not deep pits with water at the bottom, but structures with a tap or pump handle—in fact, in some parts of the country the kitchen tap is still known as a well!

The disposal of refuse was not a very strong point in Scottish burghs, and the cry of 'Gardy Loo' as some evil-smelling pitcher was tipped into the streets from an upper window was often heard. This offal was not supposed to be emptied till evening, but nevertheless it was not cleared till next morning and the condition of the streets must have been beyond belief to our modern senses. It was always a source of complaint. Even in the fifteenth century William Dunbar writes:

> May nane pas throw your principall gaittis
> For stink of haddockies and of scattis.

Dr. Johnson's remark in 1773 as Boswell armed him up the High Street of 'I smell you in the dark' is almost too well known to be repeated, and even in 1819 the poet Southey writes of 'The windes, down which an English eye may look, but into which no English nose would willing venture, for stinks older than the Union are to be found there.'

Opening from the High Street, where, as we have seen, the

tolbooth and mercat cross stood, were sometimes other streets of some importance, and they were always known, as in Sweden, as gates. Gate or gait means in Scots a way or road, hence the street leading towards the church was Kirkgate, to the Castle Castlegate, and so forth. There are Kirkgates in many towns, including Linlithgow, Leith, Burntisland, Cupar, Dunfermline, Pittenweem, Alloa, and Aberdeen, while, as at Irvine, the space in front of the church is the Kirkgatehead. The winding street to the harbour at Crail is the Shoregate, while at Montrose, Irvine, and Arbroath similar ways are known as Seagate. Ayr has its Sandgate, and Linlithgow its Watergate. In Peebles, Irvine, and Ayr the Bridge-gate leads to the respective bridges of these towns, the last so famous. At Auchtermuchty is a Gladgate, which is derived from the Gleds or hawks kept there by the Royal Falconer. There are of course many others, North and East gates in Peebles, Westgate in Dunbar, Applegate in Arbroath, Sidegate in Haddington, Bonny-gate in Cupar, Maygate in Dunfermline, Gallowgate in Glasgow and Kinghorn, Coalgate in Alloa, Wellgate in Lanark, and numbers more which are equally descriptive of their destination. A curious habit has grown up in some towns of adding the word street. This can only be taken as a sign of deplorable ignorance, for as the word gate already means a street, it is a trifle redundant to repeat the same thing in another language. Cowgates are met with in several towns, including Edinburgh, Kirkintilloch, Stonehaven, and Thurso, and are generally found to lead to the outskirts. Many people kept cows in their back premises, and every morning the town herd would collect them to drive them down the Cowgate to the common lands outside. There they grazed all day and were returned in the evening. The keeping of cows in towns was by no means confined to the seventeenth or earlier centuries. In 1786 a gentleman who has just bought a house in George Street, Edin-burgh, writes: 'we are to have a cow house and hay loft but for the present neither coach house nor stable, it is the third house west from the corner of Frederick Street.' He adds that he proposes to keep two cows, and even over fifty years after he writes, the Professions and Trades Directories of Edinburgh give a long list of names under the heading 'Cowfeeders.'

The smaller public thoroughfares were generally known as

126 The Harbour at Crail, Fife

127 Cross Wynd, Falkland, Fife

128 Ceres, Fife

Wynds or Vennels, and were often so narrow and steep that they were unfit for wheeled traffic. These lanes led to various defined places and, as with the gates, the church was often the objective, so we find that there are Kirk Wynds in numerous places, including Prestonpans, Crail, Cupar, Clackmannan, and Kirkcaldy. Kirkcaldy also contains a Coal Wynd and a Flesh Wynd, Kelso and Falkland a Mill Wynd, Montrose a Shore Wynd, Kinross and Elie a School Wynd, and Leith and Peterhead Tolbooth Wynds, all of which names explain themselves. The Vennels, from the French *venelle*, were not supposed to be the best part of the town in which to live, and they were generally narrow and dirty alleys. It is a common name, however, and though known often as the Vennel, as in Edinburgh, Dunbar, Linlithgow, and other places, there are numerous cases where it too had some qualification, for in Irvine are Glasgow and Kirk Vennels, in Ayr a Boat Vennel, Cromarty has a Big and a Little Vennel, while at Wigtown there is a High and a Low Vennel.

The smallest passages were known as closes, and usually these were private ways to one or several houses. From either side of the High Street or gates these narrow pends led under the houses into picturesque courts from which front doors opened, and beyond to gardens, kailyards or perhaps a doocot. Every community had its doocots where pigeons might grow fat for the tables of the burghers. There are still three doocots at Inverkeithing and two at St. Andrews, while in the country places many examples remain, both of the early 'beehive' type and of the later lean-to pattern.

The street entrance was closed by a yett or door which was locked at night, and at Haddington in particular nearly every close is still entered through a door. It was a good arrangement for the time, and rendered both the entrances to the houses and their plots of land comparatively safe from any disturbance in the street. The names of such closes are legion; in Edinburgh that nearest the edge of the town is known as World's End, but on the whole it was more usual to call them after the family whose house was situated therein. At Dalkeith, for instance, the existing closes are chiefly named after the people marked as their owners in a map prepared in 1822. There can be no doubt that many were airless owing to their extreme narrowness, but they are nevertheless

attractive to look upon, as may be observed at the White Horse
Close and Bakehouse Close in the Canongate of Edinburgh, Red
Lion Close in Elgin, and one near the harbour at Anstruther Easter.
Their number is often great; along the High Street of Linlithgow
alone there are still over a hundred, though they are largely rebuilt.

Few Scottish towns were walled in an extensive or military
manner. Edinburgh was one of the exceptions, and there is
evidence of a wall along the south side of the ridge at an early
date. The most famous, though, is the Flodden Wall, built after
that battle and extended later. Portions of the Edinburgh wall
may still be seen in the Vennel. Perth also was walled at one time,
and there are some remains at Stirling of a wall crowning a rocky
cliff. Though walls were not usual, the older towns were by no
means unprotected; the entrances to the burghs were all guarded
by ports (English gate or bar), a word derived from the Latin
porta and still used with the same meaning in Scandinavia. It is
most unfortunate that only one town port is still in existence. Some
were probably simple enough, but the splendid Netherbow Port of
Edinburgh removed in 1764 was a great loss to the city. It is
understandable, nevertheless, that they should have been demolished, for their narrow arch must have been a considerable hindrance
to traffic even a hundred years ago. The remaining example is the
West Port of St. Andrews, which stands at the end of South Street,
and the contract for its construction, dated 1589, is still extant. The
archway is set between two semi-octagonal towers, and the whole
crowned by a parapet. St. Andrews is also fortunate in possessing
several other ports and a great stretch of wall, but these are not
municipal, for they surround the precincts of the Cathedral and
Priory. The main gateway, in this case known as the Pends, is a
magnificent structure of the fourteenth century, which was formerly
vaulted, but the existing wall is later and was completed by Prior
Patrick Hepburn, who succeeded in 1522. It is an impressive work,
for thirteen towers still remain and two other ports besides the
Pends. However, the town ports are often commemorated by name,
and short lengths of street mark where they stood; there are West
Ports at Edinburgh, Dunbar, Linlithgow, Falkland, Lanark, and
Dysart; and East Ports at Melrose, Dunfermline, Falkland, and
Dysart, to mention only a few.

Except for the ports, there was no direct access to the streets, for the walls which bounded the private gardens ran round the town and formed an effective obstacle to all but a large organised attack. These walls were built to a considerable height and were in line with one another. Good examples may be seen at Haddington and Dunbar. Round the outside was a path, and though in many cases the path has become a busy street, the name of Back Dykes sometimes remains, as at Pittenweem, Strathmiglo, and Auchtermuchty, though it is often changed to Back Road or Street. At Banff it was known by the descriptive title of Heads of Yards, but with singular lack of imagination it has been changed to Walker Avenue—while Kelso's Back Way is now Bowmont Street. There may be reasons, financial or otherwise, for removing old houses, but there can be no reason except petty snobbery for removing old names. They mark the streets and boundaries of our old burghs in the clearest fashion, even though there may not be a single ancient building standing. Beyond the Back Dykes was the town common already mentioned. Apart from grazing, it was often the scene of sport, and there the Bow Butts were raised. Here again only the old names exist. In St. Andrews is a Butts Wynd which presumably led to the ground on the Scores, while at Tranent, Kilwinning, Montrose, Haddington, and Kelso the name Butts or Bow Butts survives.

The seaboard towns with harbours nearly always designated the street which ran by the quay as the Shore. The Shore of Leith is famous for the landings and departures of the figures who have made Scottish history, and today it is still full of interest and still dominated by the great signal tower built in 1685 as a windmill by Robert Mylne, the King's Master Mason. In those days it stood by the sea, but now the Forth is far away across the docks. Anstruther Easter, Dysart, Dunbar, Pittenweem, Banff, Cromarty, and Thurso still have their Shore, though in some cases the unnecessary title of street has been added.

Such, roughly, were the burghs till the middle of the eighteenth century, and so are many of them still. Unless the site was new, they grew along the old lines in a haphazard way. In spite of increasing prosperity, it was not usual to found entirely new towns in the eighteenth century, but the few which were are notable.

In some cases a rich lord found that a straggling village round the gates of his castle was not a good neighbour, especially if he wished to build a new house in the grand manner and lay out a park. This happened early in the century at Yester, and the village of Gifford was built. Its plan is all that could be desired. From the gates into the park a tree-lined avenue flanked with white-harled houses on one side, across a wide grass space, runs to the mercat cross and tolbooth (now rebuilt). At right angles runs another street of similar houses, terminated by a splendid church built in 1710. This church is very simple but very suitable, and with its harled walls, round-headed windows, and well-proportioned tower projecting to the street, capped by a short spire, it is a splendid piece of good manners in architecture—a focal point but by no means obtrusive. Unfortunately, within the last few years some misguided hand has daubed the white walls with a dreadful drab-colour wash—thereby destroying much of the charm of the whole village. Another example of this wholesale removal of a community is Inveraray, which dates from a few years later. Its central feature is also the church, which has a small spire and pediments supported by long thin classical columns. The houses round it are very simple, with white-harled walls and slated roofs; those standing along the shore are connected by delightful white-washed arches. The whole effect is charming, and so simple that with proper supervision it would not be beyond the pockets of the local authorities today. Good proportion and straightforward planning are quite as Scottish as turrets and dormer windows, and far more suitable to the present time. Bowmore in the Isle of Islay is slightly later, but the planning is there. From the jetty which projects into the sea a wide street of white (or once white) houses sweeps up the hill to a circular church. The only break in its round gleaming body is a tower and spire bearing a panel stating that Daniel Campbell, Lord of this island, built this church at his own charges, and dedicated it to the Supreme Deity in the year 1767.

On a larger scale the New Town of Edinburgh, which was planned in 1767, carries out the same idea, and it is for us to relearn the lesson which was well known two hundred years ago.

The houses in the earlier towns were probably mean structures built of wood and clustering near the local castle. They were

129 Inveraray, Argyll (eighteenth century)

130 Houses in Sailors' Walk, Kirkcaldy, Fife

frequently destroyed by fires both accidental and intentional, so of them nothing remains. In fact, town houses before the beginning of the seventeenth century are rather exceptional, and any built before the Reformation in 1560 are decidedly rare. There are a few in St. Andrews which are earlier, but owing to continuous occupation they have been so altered that it is impossible to be sure of their original form. The small building known as the Bishop's Palace, which stands near the west front of Elgin Cathedral, is one of the best preserved pre-Reformation houses. Part is in ruin, but the greater part is roofed, and it doubtless served as a temporary residence when the Bishop visited the Cathedral from his great Palace of Spynie, some three miles away.

One of the earlier houses remaining in Edinburgh is that known as John Knox's, which has been carefully tended in the belief that the Reformer lived therein. This is no place to discuss the matter, but, though it has been somewhat restored—the timber gables in particular—it still remains a fine specimen of its time. Among other carvings on its walls are the arms and initials of James Mosman, the goldsmith, who is known to have possessed property here in 1573. Next door, and at right angles to it, is Moubray House, another fine mansion which is carefully preserved by the Cockburn Association. It contains a good plaster ceiling and some panelling. Also in Edinburgh is Huntly House, which still retains overhanging plastered gables on a wooden framework. On a panel built into the first floor is the date 1570. This house has been purchased by the City authorities and turned into a museum, housing panelling and other fragments from properties whose fate has been less happy. The entrance is from the close behind, and there are no doors opening directly into the street. Another house with a similar entrance which, though altered, dates largely from this period is Queen Mary's House in St. Andrews. One of its most interesting features is an oriel window which projects from a corner of the upper floor of the wing. It too has fallen into good hands and has been carefully restored as the library for St. Leonard's School for Girls. In Dysart is a delightful little house standing on the shore near St. Serf's Tower. It is a simple two-storeyed block with crowstepped gables and a courtyard behind. On the lintel which gives access thereto is carved in

raised lettering 'MY . HOIP . IS . IN . THE . LORD 1583.' The local
tradition is that it was an inn, which from its proximity to the
harbour it may well have been.   This and a number of other houses
of the period would not look out of place standing by themselves
in a rural setting.   In the upper part of Dysart is a house of L plan
with a doorway in the angle and projecting upper floor to the small
wing known as the Towers which is very like a country house.
Over the doorway is the date 1589.   Queen Mary's House in
Jedburgh, now the town museum, is somewhat similar and has a
charming corbelled stair tower.   It was formerly thatched, but
before the town acquired it it was unfortunately roofed with un-
pleasant tiles quite out of keeping with the surroundings.   Still
another good specimen of this period stands in the High Street
of Pittenweem.   It is known as Kelly Lodge and is supposed to
have been the town residence of the Lairds of Kelly, whose castle
stands within a few miles.

The habit of building town houses or lodgings was very common
among the nobility of the late sixteenth and early seventeenth centuries.   The finest, as is natural, are to be found in Edinburgh and
Stirling; in fact, the Argyll Lodging in Stirling is the largest town
house in Scotland.   It is now a military hospital, but the exterior
is little touched since it was built by the Earl of Stirling in 1630
and finished by the Argyll family who acquired it some years later.
In plan it is somewhat like the letter E, with two wings projecting
from the main block to the street and there joined by a high wall
pierced by an archway to form a courtyard.   The windows are
surmounted by strapwork pediments, and the stair towers with
their high pointed roofs make a rich and fine composition.   Near
it are the ruins of Mars Work, which has been a large house of
rather earlier date, having been built in 1570 by the Earl of Mar
who was Regent of Scotland.   Its entrance was through an arch
flanked by semi-octagonal towers, and the street elevation is notable
for the number of carved stones and rich mouldings.   There are
also several inscriptions, one of which is a delightful invitation to
architectural critics:

'I PRAY AL LUIKARIS ON THIS LUGING
WITH GENTIL E TO GIF THAIR JUDGING'

though whatever the critic was bold enough to say about it to the great man was not likely to make much impression, for a further couplet in the courtyard runs:

'ESSPY . SPEIK . FURTH . AND SPAIR . NOTHT
CONSIDDER . VEIL . I . CAIR . NOTHT'.

The great lodgings of the nobility at Edinburgh were chiefly in the Canongate, which was then a separate burgh, whose tolbooth has been already mentioned. It was not so closely built as Edinburgh itself; there was space for large gardens sloping southward and facing the Salisbury Crags; furthermore, it lay nearer the Palace. One of the finest of these mansions is Moray House, which is now used as a Training College. It was built in the 1620's by Mary, Dowager Countess of Home, and her initials may still be seen over one of the windows. As in the earlier houses, there is no door directly opening on to the street, but instead of going through a pend there is a splendid gateway with high pyramidal tops to the posts and a porter's lodge at one side. Over the street projects a balcony supported by carved brackets, and the whole composition is more Renaissance in feeling than those mentioned above. The interior still contains magnificent vaulted plaster ceilings with most elaborate details.

In Bakehouse Close behind Huntly House is Acheson House, which conforms rather more to the Scottish tradition. It was built in 1633, according to the date carved over the door, which opens into a small courtyard screened from the close by a wall. Owing to many years of misuse its interior retains little of its old decoration, but thanks to the Marquess of Bute it has now (1938) been restored.

The nobility were not the only people to have town houses, for many of the small burghs have mansions which belonged to the local lairds, even though their country seats were only a mile or two away. Kelly Lodge at Pittenweem was one; the house of the Hendersons at Inverkeithing with its picturesque corbelled round or tower another, though the family home, Fordell Castle, is under two miles away. The Inverkeithing house is now well preserved as a church hall. Even nearer was Coates House, which stands in the shadow of St. Mary's Cathedral in Edinburgh and was built by John Byres in 1615. It is only three-quarters of a mile from West Port, but nevertheless the family had a lodging of some sort in Byres Close. Among other such houses remaining are those of the Hamiltons of Humbie and Pardovan in the High Street of Linlithgow, of the Holborns of Menstrie in Inverkeithing, of the Lovats in Inverness, the Duffs of Braco in Elgin, Balmerino and Preston of Airdrie in Cupar, Glencairn at Dumbarton, and many more in such centres as Banff, Aberdeen, St. Andrews, Perth, Ayr, and Kirkcudbright. Most of them are quite small and were doubtless only used for business and for the short 'seasons' which these places would afford.

The main bulk of the town houses were erected by the merchants, the guilds, and the smaller craftsmen. In Edinburgh the great flatted tenements known as 'Lands' are a feature of the High Street and Canongate. Gladstone Land in the Lawnmarket, built by Thomas Gladstone in 1631, is a fine example. Its ground floor is arcaded, and five more storeys rise above it to picturesque gables.* On the opposite side of the street is the rather earlier house of the wealthy Bailie Macmorran tucked away down a close and built round a small court. Inside are good panelling and fine plaster ceilings. In the Canongate are the Morocco, Shoemakers' and Golfers' Lands, all characteristic tall buildings, and all with romantic stories. Other places were not so crowded as Edinburgh, and it is not common to find houses of such height, three or, at the outside, four floors being the usual limit. The nine and ten storeys in Edinburgh were unusual anywhere in these days, and were nearly always commented upon by travellers.

One of the finest houses erected by a merchant in the early seventeenth century was the so-called Palace at Culross. This quiet little town was then a busy industrial centre with an extensive trade in coal and salt. It furthermore had the monopoly of making girdles, which were one of the few really indispensable utensils of the Scottish kitchen. The town has lost its trade but fortunately kept its old houses. Still more fortunately, the National Trust for Scotland has purchased a great many of them, so that it should stand for years to come as a well-nigh perfect example of a small

* This house has been acquired by the National Trust for Scotland and is now undergoing a judicious restoration. Several fine painted ceilings have been found in process of the work.

133 Huntly House from Bakehouse Close

132 The West Bow

EDINBURGH, THE OLD TOWN

131 Fisher's Close

135 Moubray House and John Knox's House
(sixteenth century)

134 Canongate Tolbooth (1591)

EDINBURGH, THE OLD TOWN

Scottish trading burgh. The Palace, one of the houses acquired by the Trust, has been carefully restored and its terraced gardens filled with flowers. It is placed in irregular fashion on two sides of a courtyard, and was built between 1597 and 1611 by George Bruce, later Lord Carnock. Its pantiled roofs and many dormer windows are typical, but the superb painted rooms inside, though perhaps typical once, are now pretty well unique. Not only the ceilings but the walls are covered with decoration, giving a rich effect which is hardly associated with the Scotland of the day. Among the other old houses near it is the Study, whose picturesque stair tower and crowstepped gables have been an inspiration to numerous artists.

The Guilds or Corporations built various meeting-places and charitable institutions, some of which remain. The Candlemakers' Hall, preserved by the City of Edinburgh, is one, and the Tailors' Hall in the same town another. An inscription on a door lintel of the latter, dated 1621, runs:

TO THE GLORIE·OF GOD·AND VERTEWIS·RENOWNE·

THE CWMPANIE·OF·TAILZEOVRS WITHIN THIS GOOD·TOVNE,

FOR MEITING·OF·THAIR·CRAFT·THIS·HAL HES·ERECTED·

IN TRVST·IN·GODS·GOODNES TO·BE·BLIST AND·PROTECTED.

The fate of this fine building is unfortunately in some doubt, but it is good news to learn that it will not be demolished. A little farther along the Cowgate is the Magdalen Chapel, which was the meeting-place of the Incorporation of Hammermen. Their insignia, a hammer surmounted by a crown, appears in several places, and the walls are lined with the painted records of benefactions. In Banff is a fine eighteenth-century house with a panel stating it was built for charitable ends in 1710, and beneath, another inscription that it was 'REBUILT BY THE INCORPORATION OF SHOEMAKERS 1787.' Heriot's Hospital in Edinburgh, the finest example of Scots Renaissance during the first half of the seventeenth century, was a private benefaction of George Heriot, goldsmith to James VI, and Cowan's Hospital in Stirling, a charming building erected in 1639, was likewise provided for by John Cowan, Dean of Guild.

The houses mentioned so far have been of some importance, but the smaller and simpler types naturally form the majority, though, owing to the present unsatisfactory conditions, they are vanishing every day. This state of affairs is much to be regretted, for a town cannot retain its charm or tradition if its buildings are all swept away except perhaps one of the more elaborate houses left jammed between a bank and a multiple store whose scale is quite out of sympathy with it. Many of them could well be reconditioned according to the regulations of the Department of Health and, as has been proved, used again for housing.

The usual, in fact universal, material of which their walls are built is local rubble, and this was always harled or roughcast and whitewashed. There was little of the gloomy dirty grey to which we are now so used, and the rows of white houses must have been cheerful and pleasant to look upon. A rare example of a finely pointed ashlar front stands in the Kirkgate of Alloa, but the fact that it was built in 1695 by Thomas Beauchop, who was master mason at the great Renaissance house of Kinross and also of the Midsteeple of Dumfries, explains this unusual feature. The roofing varied according to the district. Thatch was probably the oldest, and till a hundred years ago was partly used in many districts. Now, however, it has all but died out except for a few places in the Howe of Fife. There are still nearly fifty thatched houses in Auchtermuchty, and a few remain in the neighbouring towns of Strathmiglo, Falkland, and Newburgh. This survival is doubtless due to the proximity of the famous reeds in the Tay. Slate is most commonly used, and there were many more quarries in existence. Stobo in Peeblesshire supplied a wide district in the south, and Aberfoyle in the centre. West Highland slates from Easdale and Ballachulish were also taken long distances. Fife and the Lothians and a large part of the East Coast imported the idea of pantiles from the Low Countries in the sixteenth and seventeenth centuries, and they are the most typical roofing material of that area, the shores of the Forth in particular. In Angus were heavy stone slates, as also in parts of Dumfriesshire, where they were of large size and sometimes hung diagonally. Thin-split Caithness flags formed many of the roofs in Thurso and Wick, though their chief use for export was paving and at one time many cargoes were sent to London. The older houses were often set side by side so that their gables faced the street. Many of these may be seen in Kirkwall, Falkland, Burntisland, and Montrose. Pennant writes in 1772: 'The houses are of stone, and like those in Flanders, often with their gable ends towards the streets.' During the seventeenth century the gables were steeply pitched, but by the end of the eighteenth became considerably lower. Their most characteristic feature is the crowstepping. Before the Reformation the steps were sometimes very large, and often, especially in the houses of church dignitaries, each was finished with a gabled cope. Several examples of these may be seen in South Street, St. Andrews, and at the Bishop's Palaces in Elgin and Dornoch. This extravagant construction died out soon after 1560, and for about two hundred years the familiar little crowsteps reigned supreme. For cottages, in fact, they did not die out till the early nineteenth century. A large house in Kirkintilloch dated 1764 has three crowstepped gables, but owing to the rather flat pitch of the roof they are not entirely satisfactory. It is interesting to see the regret with which they were given up, for in many places the half of the gable to the street has a straight skew and the other half is crowstepped. Sometimes in the later seventeenth and early eighteenth centuries gables were curved in a simple version of the Dutch manner. It was not very common but there are examples at Inveresk, Leven, Banff, and Pittenweem.

In some towns the houses in the principal streets are arcaded and the fronts supported on arches. There are several with remains of this treatment in Elgin, the best preserved being the house of Duff of Braco dated 1694, where the arches are now utilised as shop windows. Dr. Johnson in his version of the tour of the Western Isles in 1773 writes that 'In the chief street of Elgin, the houses jut over the lowest story, like the old buildings of timber in London, but with greater projections; so that there is sometimes a walk for a considerable length under a cloister, or portico, which is now indeed frequently broken, because the new houses have another form, but it seems to have been uniformly continued in the old city.' Parts of Glasgow were similarly treated, and Pennant in 1772 notes that 'many of the houses are built over arcades, but too narrow to be walked in with any conveniency.'

These houses were functional in the true sense of the word and decoration was used sparingly; some have picturesque stair

S

turrets, but for the most part they are quite plain and rely on their excellent proportions of windows, door, and roof. The doorways are sometimes well moulded, and at all periods lintels carved with dates or initials are common; above is, if the owner were entitled thereto, a panel containing his coat of arms. The windows are simple rectangular openings, often surrounded in later examples by a slightly raised margin against which the harling was stopped. Till the middle of the seventeenth century the opening was divided in half by a wooden transom, below which were shutters which could be opened for ventilation, while above was fixed glass—in the earlier examples leaded and run direct into a groove in the stonework, in the later framed in wood with astragals. The sash and case window then came in, though it was some time before the upper sash was made to move. The casement window has never been popular in Scotland. Dormer windows are frequent, and those of the earlier seventeenth century are very pleasing, with every variety of pediment carved with the owner's arms, initials, and dates. Another feature often seen adorning the fronts of these houses is the sundial, which may be built into a corner, project on a carved bracket, stand on the crowsteps, or even form part of a chimney. Many are most ingenious, with two if not three faces, each with a different-shaped gnomon and a different method of throwing the shadow. Many are dated, and they seem to have been most common from the middle of the seventeenth to the middle of the eighteenth centuries, though they often occur both earlier and later.

The inscriptions and dates on these buildings form an interesting study. As already mentioned, the date was often on the lintel, but it varies to a certain extent throughout the country. In some places, as Airth, the date and initials are all carved on small square panels over the door, while at Kincardine-on-Forth, only two miles away, this is rare and the date is in most cases carved directly on to the lintel. Kincardine is also notable for the number of its dated houses, and the tradition there carried on well into the nineteenth century. In other places the fashion seemed to be to put dates and initials on the skewputt, that is, the lowest stone of a crow-stepped gable, which generally projected and was carved on the under-side. This habit is used to a limited extent in a number of

138 Arcaded House, Elgin

137 Tain Tolbooth, Ross

FEATURES OF THE BURGH

136 Close in Anstruther Easter, Fife

139 Detail of Dormer Windows

140 West Wing

CULROSS PALACE, FIFE

towns, but is very common in Elgin, Irvine, and Kilwinning. In some burghs very few houses are dated, for doubtless the fashion depended much upon the local masons and whether they enjoyed a bit of 'fancy work' to show their skill. Before around 1680 the lettering was always raised, and though it was more labour the builders inclined to be more verbose. Pious mottoes in Latin and Scots were long a favourite subject. 'NISI DOMINUS FRUSTRA' appears often, while at Kilwinning we get 'GOD IS THE BUILDER PRAESIT BE HE'; in Peebles as late as 1716 'IN DEO EST OMNIA FIDES'; in 1641 at South Queensferry 'SPES MEA CHRISTUS'; at Kincardine-on-Forth in the early seventeenth century 'GOD IS MY LYF MY LAND AND RENT HIS PROMIS IS MY EVIDENT' and he defiantly ends with 'LAT THEM SAY.' As behoved a house standing beneath the walls of a Royal Palace, we get delightful inscriptions from Falkland, one of which runs: 'AL PRAISE TO GOD AND THANKS TO THE MOST EXCELLENT MONARCHE GREAT BRITANE OF WHOSE PRINCELIE LIBERALITIE THIS IS MY PARTIOUNE DEO LAVS ESTO FIDVS ADEST MERCES NICOLL MONCRIEF 1610;' and next door one on the same lines: 'I . R . 6 . GOD SAIF YE KING OF GRIT BRITAIN FRANCE AND IRLAND OUR SOVERAN FOR OF HIS LIBERALITY THIS HOUSE DID I EDIFY.' Such orations were not very usual in the eighteenth century, and at that time the commonest date-stone was the so-called marriage-lintel, which was generally arranged thus: 17 IS . TK 72, with the lettering incised. The initials were those of the owner and his wife, who always in Scotland, even on her tombstone, kept her maiden name. Between the two sets of initials a heart is sometimes carved, or sometimes, if a seaman, an anchor; if a merchant, his mark, which was like the figure 4; if a joiner, his square; or the hammer and crown of the hammerman or smith, or the shovel of the maltster. These stones, of course, commemorated the building of the house and not necessarily the date of marriage. For instance, at Ceres in Fife is a lintel inscribed $16^{WT}_{EA}85$, while on a more modern and commodious house alongside is 17 WT EA 14, which shows the worthy couple had prospered. In the same village the addition to a house has the husband's initials only and a date twenty-six years later than the lintel with the combined initials, so we may presume that his spouse had died meanwhile. Occasionally people had their names written in full, as on a panel at Dunfermline dated 1745 where the son's name is also added; while at North Queensferry, carved on a house rather more ostentatious than the others, is 'B. DRUMMOND, VINTNER JANU 17TH 1766.' These dates and initials generally interest the occupiers, but recently an owner in South Queensferry had several fine seventeenth-century-dated lintels chiselled down in order that prospective tenants might imagine the houses to be modern, which a glance at the houses would show to be a curiously ignorant hope.

All these little things add vastly to the interest of Scottish burghs, but such houses are vanishing every day. The local authorities are pleased to say that they will preserve anything of architectural interest, which means that such lintels and date-panels will be built into the walls of a gawky council house. There is no point in a seventeenth or eighteenth century stone in such a setting; that isn't architectural interest! Architecture goes much farther than that: she does not dot random old stones in new buildings, but treats the buildings as a whole. Not only the build-ings but the whole town must be properly planned so that each house is in harmony with its neighbours; the churches and public buildings should dominate, but must also be good companions, not looking down on their humbler neighbours with a haughty stare from their vacant plate-glass windows.

There is a fund of good sense and good manners to be learnt by the study of the old Scottish burghs, but few realise this wider application; we have a sad complex of inferiority and cannot imagine that these old houses can be beautiful in themselves. If Mary Queen of Scots has stayed in one of them it is of interest; pull the others down—who is B. Drummond, Vintner, anyway? This attitude is all too common, though there are exceptions and the exceptions are increasing. Stirling Burgh, with the help of the Thistle Trust, is endeavouring to save every old building possible and insisting that the new ones must be in scale and harmony. They see the need for progress as well as anyone else—and perhaps better, for they are not going to spoil one of their great assets as a tourist centre without thought; and having taken thought, they find that there is no need to spoil that asset. This is the secret, for no one wishes to preserve anything that is quite impossible to make into a satisfactory modern house, but some more consideration would have undoubtedly saved much that has gone. Crail is another burgh whose Council has passed resolutions to safeguard its old houses and is trying to interest the owners in the preservation of their property. They too see that it is a priceless asset to pass on to their descendants.

In all fairness, the local authorities are in some difficulty, for the Government do not allow any grant for reconditioning old houses in urban areas, but do for building new ones. The easiest way out is, therefore, to accept the grant, demolish existing property and rebuild, for the apathy in Scotland today is so great that most people cannot be bothered to make a stand or to think about anything unless it affects their personal comfort. If, however, combined pressure were used, the Government might well alter matters —in fact, there are already signs of a very cautious yielding in this direction. The majority of our larger monuments are already under the care of the Ancient Monuments Department of the Office of Works, but this body cannot undertake the reconditioning or ownership of more than a limited number of monuments. For another thing, their houses are bound by law to be show-places, and the only inhabitants allowed are caretakers. This is of course an impossible position, for, except in a few special cases, it is most undesirable that our houses should be other than lived in. Further, the Commissioners are not empowered to take over buildings later in date than 1707, which excludes a vast number of the simple houses in the burghs, and, in any case, even then they are handicapped by lack of funds. The National Trust for Scotland has a wider policy, and having renovated properties can let them to suitable tenants. However, since this body depends entirely on voluntary donations, it is impossible for it to take the matter up in the national manner required. They are doing good work, though. Culross and Gladstone Land have both been mentioned, and they are also restoring a group of fine houses in the Sailors' Walk at Kirkcaldy, Hugh Millar's birthplace in Cromarty, Stenhouse Mills near Edinburgh, and the Hamilton Dower House at Preston. Lists are being prepared on their behalf of all the old town houses in Scotland; these are sent to the Department of Health, with whose co-operation and that of the Office of Works they hope to be able to rouse the authorities to their responsibilities. Local preservation trusts are springing up at St. Andrews and Falkland. The latter have already purchased a fine group of small houses in Cross Wynd which will be carefully renovated. All this, coupled with the generous efforts of private individuals, is undoubtedly awakening interest, and also a realisation of the possibilities and value of these old houses.

141 The Old Brig at Stirling (fifteenth century)

142 Fireplace, Carriston Castle, Brechin.   The ornament of the early
Renaissance

Ian C. Hannah

~~~~~~

TRIUMPHANT CLASSICISM

~~~~~~

A MOST bumptious and objectionable man was Robert Cochrane, a fellow of low birth and high conceit whom, in defiance of all the traditions of the royal house, James III had made his closest friend. Far and wide the fellow had travelled; on the Continent he had spent much time, and in the Italy of the early Renaissance he had picked up the most absurd ideas. His manners were utterly intolerable, his dress was outlandish and loud, his conceit was such as no sane mortal could endure. The air of absurd superiority that he assumed among the ancient nobility was trying to the last degree, and when his royal master dubbed him Earl of Mar the wrath of the Scots peers boiled.

They found it exceedingly difficult to restrain the righteous indignation that they felt. It must be admitted that they did not try very hard, but under the leadership of Bell-the-Cat—Archibald Douglas, the Earl of Angus—they hanged him from Lauder bridge, scoffing at his last request that they would use a silken cord.

This early instance of lynch law took place in 1482, and that was three years before, upon the field of Bosworth, the splendour-loving Tudor house got possession of the English throne. Doubtless the feelings of the Scottish lairds were suitably relieved, and they had not the faintest suspicion that they had abruptly put a term to one of the most outstanding careers connected with British

103

architecture. For this Cochrane had (almost undoubtedly) designed for his royal friend the stately hall of Stirling Castle, the first building, as it appears, in the whole of the British Isles that displays any Renaissance influence. We may study it today, for its thick walls still stand firm, though its whole inside is gutted and very clumsily reconstructed as an ordinary barrack block.

Thus the new architectural tradition came to Scotland very early indeed, not to destroy the ancient Gothic style but rather to fulfil— for long years, in fact, merely to give to the old and massive forms new detail that might a little differently set off the character of a window or a parapet or a door: little more. The general appearance was but slightly affected. And yet a new thing had come which was at last to leaven and remake the whole. As in England and the north of Europe generally, the earliest Renaissance forms are grafted almost imperceptibly on to the old vernacular style. Classic details creep in, but the Gothic lines remain. The general effect is very much the same. This may be studied in most important Scottish buildings between the reigns of James IV and Charles II.

A little later than Cochrane's hall, indeed, two noble buildings rose, very much in the style of the continental Renaissance—in the fashions of Italy and France—one close beside the hall on Stirling hill, the other in the plain of Fife at Falkland; but these are almost wanderers from the banks of Arno and of Loire, they had but little influence on the general development of Scotland's art.

It was a Scottish king, James VI-I, who at Whitehall employed Inigo Jones to erect the first uncompromisingly classic building that the British Isles ever saw—the banqueting-hall that was to have formed part of a perfectly enormous palace (p. 106); but this was not followed up in England for a full generation, while Scotland saw nothing of the like till the very end of the seventeenth century. This triumphant classic style, in England and Scotland alike, marks a break with the past that is almost complete. It is definitely an importation from the south. It is unrelated to what has gone before, and yet it is in logical sequence with the first introduction of Renaissance forms. The whole lines of buildings are altered; their character is completely changed. And yet historic continuity is not entirely lost. In Scotland the transition is perhaps more gradual than in England, though the definitely undiluted classic buildings—such as Kinross House or the nave of St. Nicholas', Aberdeen, are just as unlike the vernacular that went before in Scotland as they are quite different from English Jacobean work. The exchange was by no means an advantage to Scotland. She lost what was wholly her own; what she gained is shared with the whole of western Europe, and to the pure classic tradition it must at once be admitted that Scotland had but little contribution to make (p. 107). A charming picturesqueness of outline, lofty roofs with perching dormers, and boldly corbelled far-over-sailing towers, exactly suited to our landscapes and part of Scotland's very soul, are sacrificed; in exchange we get a rather ordinary version of the general tradition of contemporary Europe, with little real adaptation to the Scottish scene.

In itself the style is very noble, and it exactly matched the times. It was entirely fit that Roman fabrics should be built of massive ashlar while Johnson, Gibbon, Hume, and many more, were writing heavy English prose in a half-Latin style. And Boswell's immortal *Life of Johnson* witnesses that Scotland's contribution to the Augustan age of Britain was by no means small. In literature it was greater than in art. Vanbrugh's career is witness that the two were closely parallel. Perhaps his work on paper justified the spirit of his famous epitaph as fully as his work in stone:

> Lie heavy on him, Earth, for he
> Laid many a heavy load on thee.

It was exceedingly fortunate that the temples, basilicas, villas, baths, and aqueducts of Rome had no place in the eighteenth century, and that therefore direct copying was impossible. The porticoes and colonnades of antiquity could, of course, be borrowed, but it was absolutely necessary to recast the designs and evolve new forms. This on the whole was done very worthily, and if one regrets that the classic style displaced the native Scottish forms, it is very largely because Corinthian porticoes require the blue skies and sunshine of the south, while the Scottish vernacular was admirably fitted to the grey skies and the twilight of a northern winter. Icicles pendant from acanthus leaves look somewhat out of place.

The gradual character of the transition in Scotland is well illustrated by such mansions as Prestonfield and Caroline Park, both of them in the suburbs of Edinburgh. It is in rather startling con-

T

trast with the way in which sixty years earlier Inigo Jones' classic palace had been rising in Whitehall at the very time that Gothic was being most effectively resuscitated at Oxford. Royston or Caroline Park was begun by George Mackenzie, first Viscount Tarbat, in 1685, and he built the northern part of the quadrangle, facing the Forth. The exterior is very plain, notably the façade, which looks north and in the lower storey has no window at all. The walls are harled and surmounted by the usual huge Scottish chimney-stacks, completely unadorned, in the old vernacular style. But the southern façade, dated 1696, is built in solid ashlar with bold pilasters, having alternate cushion stones, and this part would be purely classic but for the ogee lines of the slated roofs of the projecting towers, which give a vernacular effect.

Prestonfield is nearly square and, rising four stages with attic above, has much of the old tower form characteristic of a common type of Scottish castle. The walls are harled with ashlar quoins of buckle form, the windows are of the traditional rectangular shape, and the gables display the curving lines of the Dutch. One of the attics gives the date, 1687. Several rooms have panelling in Memel pine, recalling the old days of Scotland's Baltic trade. One chamber has stamped leather walls in rather high relief. The front stair has a short wall with rounded ends in place of the older newel-post, a very common Scottish way of getting easier treads. All this is in the vernacular tradition with Low Country influence, but in the drawing-room—Scots-like, upon an upper floor— are bold bolection mouldings and ceiling panels worked out in high and masculine relief in the style of triumphant classicism.

But both these houses are most interesting for their plaster-work in very high relief, displaying at Prestonfield grotesque heads, lions, cherubs, birds, fruit and foliage, rich and unrestrained, and above what was originally a stair-head hangs a detached pendant cherub. At Caroline Park the two chief apartments have fine panelled plaster ceilings whose thick ribs display the usual classic form of flowers and foliage and fruit. They enclose paintings by N. Hevde representing Aurora, and Diana visiting Endymion. In both mansions, too, paintings are inset in the panelling that sheathes the walls.

This work, which comparatively is on a small scale, is of great interest as representing the manner in which the baroque flood,

144 Screen Doors, Foulis Easter, Fife

143 Staircase, Caroline Park, Midlothian

145 Hopetoun House, West Lothian. Begun by Sir William Bruce in 1696

146 Gosford House, East Lothian. Begun by Robert Adam

rising in the south of Europe, ebbed against the shores of Scotland. This was essentially the style of the counter-Reformation and of the new Jesuit order. It is the fashion to belittle it, but such fashions may pass away. Its great merit was that it enabled different countries to give their own atmosphere to a classic tradition that otherwise was monotonously uniform. We see it in Venice and other towns of Italy rioting in the most exuberant though purely European ornament; in the two Americas, chiefly in their tropical highlands, it flames in soaring detail borrowed from ancient Indian art, and Christian saints stand out in the forms, and to a great extent amid the surroundings, of the discarded Aztec gods; in Prague and Krakow great baroque churches weirdly eschew straight lines, and their enormous façades and colonnades writhe in snake-like, most unrestful curves. British objections to the style were by no means purely religious; even St. Paul's displays a few timid details that if magnified and emphasised would give a baroque air. The truth is exactly expressed in the best criticism of Britain that a foreigner has recently penned: 'No style is more alien to English taste than the baroque, with its large and often meaningless gestures, its florid and frequently poor materials. Baroque exaggerates; the Englishman understates. Baroque dramatises; the Englishman is untheatrical in all things.'* This is at least equally true of the Scot.

Baroque ruled out, there was virtually no scope for any real Scottish development of the classic style. We shall see that the northern kingdom made no small contribution to the best English work of the eighteenth century, but one can hardly speak of any Scottish school. The architecture of the two countries had been steadily drawing apart since the end of the fourteenth century; it now became more uniform than ever since Norman times.†

England was most fortunate during the seventeenth century in being served by two of the greatest masters of all time, Inigo Jones and Sir Christopher Wren. The day of architects had fully come, for the old tradition of communal building was very largely past. Elizabethan mansions for the most part had been designed by individuals. Scotland had to be content to see the classic style introduced by a good though, it must be admitted, a rather ordinary

---

* *Those English*, by Kurt von Stutterheim (Sidgwick & Jackson, 1937), p. 140.
† This must be understood of important buildings; of cottages it is much less true.

architect, Sir William Bruce of Kinross. He died at an advanced age in 1710, and so is exactly contemporary with Wren. Like Cochrane, he was immersed in high affairs of state; he took a leading Scottish part in the Restoration of 1660, and was quite as prominent as almost any one of his day in public life. He was a man of scholarly tastes, and if he is perhaps a little lacking in the originality and resourcefulness that display themselves so strikingly in the works of Wren, his buildings have dignity and power.

Both Inigo Jones and Wren were steeped in the Gothic tradition, however much they had made themselves masters of the Italian school. In many of the works of Jones, notably his reconstruction of Ford Abbey in Dorset, this is very clear, and he sometimes built in the Gothic style, as in the chapel of Lincoln's Inn. Wren's Gothic buildings are well known, and they have real charm though they look as though he were thinking of classic all the time. String-courses almost become cornices; the lines are chiefly horizontal. Even St. Paul's, the noblest of all the great churches of the Renaissance, with its nave-long quire and long-drawn aisles, has an interior of Gothic mystery and gloom, while study reveals concealed flying buttresses and discloses the fact that the dome on its eight great arches exactly reproduces the arrangement of the fourteenth-century octagon at Ely. (Wren was a nephew of its bishop.)

Thus it should be no surprise to find that Sir William Bruce, if at Hopetoun and Kinross itself he has left work uncompromisingly classic, was yet impregnated with the Scottish tradition and often carried on the spirit of the vernacular. At times indeed we find him in the grip of the seventeenth-century desire to restore a pure Gothic, which, chiefly centred in Oxford and Northamptonshire, had spread into the Scotland of a generation or so earlier than his. (Prominent examples are Greyfriars' and the Tron Kirk in Edinburgh, the parish churches of South Queensferry, Dairsie in Fife, Lyne in Peeblesshire, the upper part of the steeple at Cupar, Fife, dated 1620, and a window at Yester with date 1635.)

Bruce's chief Gothic fabric is the Merchants' House tower at Glasgow, one of his early works. The lower part is plain and stands four-square; two upper stages get narrower at each remove, and parapets surround their bases and also the top, within which rises the spire. The lower of these upper storeys has double

lancets; the higher, windows of three lights, the mullions intersecting in the heads—a form that in England was evolved in the
late thirteenth century and reappears about the very end of the
fifteenth, but in Scotland it is very usual at all periods. The
skyline of this steeple is very good, but fortunately its style was
never followed up. The classicism that was now triumphant
throughout the entire west of Europe offered better things.

In 1671 Bruce was appointed king's surveyor, and in that
capacity at once set about the reconstruction of Holyrood House.
Despite its associations, this was far from being the finest Scottish
royal dwelling at the time. Like Dunfermline and Arbroath, it had
originated from the fondness of the Scottish monarchs for the
society of monks, prompting them to construct royal lodgings
within the precincts of convents. But the castle of Edinburgh had
never been entirely supplanted; it saw the birth of James VI.
Royal dwellings were rather numerous, but, except perhaps at
Linlithgow, had little of the stately splendour that was looked for
in the south. And, though he cannot be said to have shown any
special attachment to Scotland, Charles II was anxious to be worthily
lodged in her capital.

Bruce's task at Holyrood was by no means easy, for he had to
incorporate older buildings which fitted badly with any ideal of
what a great classic palace should be. The glorious nave of the
old Augustinian church, one of the most splendid works that
thirteenth-century Scotland produced, had become the chapel
royal, and, as the west claustral buildings had occupied the site
to be taken by the east side of the new quadrangle, it grouped very
badly indeed; in fact, the palace could only find room after the
destruction of the projecting south-west tower of the nave, a most
serious loss to the church. About 1528 James V had erected, a
little to the south-west of the west façade of the church, a characteristic heavy oblong four-storey tower with huge round corner
turrets, the building that had seen most of the deathless romance
connected with the names of Queen Mary, Darnley, Rizzio, and
John Knox. For the sake of classic symmetry a duplicate was now
(1671-79) erected some distance to the south, but on a far less
massive plan. These two form the familiar far-projecting wings of
the west front of the existing building. While the three other sides

of the quadrangle have three storeys with attic, the west side is kept low with a central columned gate over which rises an octagonal clock tower, bearing the date 1680. The court is surrounded by a heavy cloister of nine round arches on each side, opening to the central space, and the two floors above have Ionic and Corinthian pilasters. The east (garden) front has similar arrangements of pilasters (Tuscan, Ionic, and Corinthian), along the sides returned for three bays round the ends; the sides otherwise are plainer. The cornices and other details are rather light, and as the towers with their wide round turrets, effectively spired, dominate nearly every view, the general effect has more of the older vernacular than that of the later classic. This impression is increased by the absence of a parapet (beyond the towers) and the way in which the dormered roofs and the chimneys are emphasised in the ancient Scottish manner. New classicism would have had them concealed, or at any rate largely masked. Standing immediately below the towering mass of Arthur's Seat and surrounded by beautiful gardens, the palace presents a general impression that is exceedingly satisfactory. The fabric possesses a sort of cultured and refined individuality which can hardly be claimed for the great contemporary palaces of the mainland, though one of them is renowned Versailles. On one of the pillars of the cloister is incised the name of Robert Mylne, who acted as master mason.

The state apartments on the east side, hung with magnificent tapestry, ceiled with designs of fruit and flowers in fairly high relief, framing rather ordinary paintings, are a most striking example of the restraint with which Scotland could treat the *motifs* of baroque. Exaggeration is entirely eschewed, and yet the effect of splendour almost unrestrained is by no means wholly lost. The Dutch painter, Jacob de Witt, who was responsible for many of the pictures at Holyrood, is seen to better advantage in the little house chapel at Glamis, the whole of whose ceiling and walls are covered.

As a master of triumphant classicism Bruce is perhaps best studied in the mansion which he erected soon after 1681 on his own estate of Kinross, a building which might stand as a monument of the Renaissance in any country of western Europe. In form it is an oblong rectangle with wings that slightly project, the whole of

147 Heriot's Hospital, Edinburgh. Begun in 1628 and completed in 1650

148 The Palace of Holyroodhouse, Edinburgh. The present palace was
designed by Sir William Bruce

149 Detail of plaster-work, Palace of Holyroodhouse

150 Ceiling, Palace of Holyroodhouse

excellent ashlar. The basement has channelled blocks; Corinthian pilasters at the angles give importance to the two main storeys and support a noble entablature, over which, just under the eaves, are the windows of what would naturally be the attic. The great hipped roof in the manner of Scotland is flat in the centre, a very questionable advantage in a land of heavy snows. There is a central cupola and the chimneys are very prominent. Without any very striking originality, the design is most effective and beautiful. From the ends of the west or front façade project two curving screens that terminate in pavilions with roofs of ogee form. This arrangement is extended by walls which enclose a vast stretch of verdure, and behind them are great masses of trees that recall the formal forest glades of France. These extend along the same lines on the far side of the house, whose windows look out between them across a formal garden, to the island castle of Loch Leven and the rugged hills beyond. This combination of formal planning with highland landscapes is very definitely Scots, and incomparably more satisfying than the formal avenues of France with only fountains at their ends.

This union of architecture and of landscape gardening is a foreign importation to Scotland. Her most distinctive mansions, such as Glamis or Fyvie, make no such effort to transform their surroundings, and yet in a sense are possessed of far greater charm. In them we seem to see the very soul of Scotland; in these she has little that is truly and indisputably her own. The older mansions are largely in the north; pure classicism is chiefly in the south.

Bruce's work is seen, on a yet vaster scale than at Kinross, on the southern banks of the Forth where at Hopetoun in 1696 he began one of the largest of all the country houses of Scotland. This one also looks both from front and rear over great glades walled by long lines of trees, and from all the front rooms of the house the curving girders of the famous bridge are seen. The front is very long and very narrow, supplemented at the back by a square block, in the centre of which is the stair, under a glass cupola. There is a bold plinth-basement with channelled joints, and at the back two storeys with attic above, ashlar throughout. Along the front façade the attic becomes a further storey, above the cornice. There are Corinthian pilasters with a stately central stairway to the door. A balustrade surmounted by urns seeks in a rather English way to conceal the chimneys and the roof. The façade is a fine composition but rather too suggestive of a screen, especially as the ends bend out, just a little awkwardly, by means of curving bays, and the transition from attic behind to extra storey in front is made with little skill. The central windows are round-headed, the others square. From the ends (but strangely out of relation to the façade) sweep forward long bending Tuscan colonnades to connect the mansion with square wings upon whose walls they are continued with pilasters in place of the free-standing pillars. These wings are surmounted by cupolas, and though for perfect symmetry they are made to look identical, they turn out to be stable and ball-room, the last with billiard-hall attached.

The whole mansion is largely sacrificed to this great long front, which is perhaps the finest of its kind in Scotland; the setting is perfectly magnificent and the general effect is very stately. (Too many of Scotland's best classic fabrics, notably the old quadrangle of Edinburgh University, suffer from their wretched sites.) The apartments of the interior are large and impressive, displaying rather ordinary classic detail worked out in white and gold; for the most part the relief of plaster detail is low, and over the bold cornices the ceilings curve upward to their flat centres. The staircase and the ball-room have good panelling with festoons of flowers and fruit in high relief, displaying Grinling Gibbons' style, but the carving is not first-rate.

There can be no doubt that Hopetoun House suffers from the fact that, left unfinished at Bruce's death, the works were continued (very slowly) by his pupil, William Adam of Maryburgh (d. 1748). He was far less able than his master, and his fame has been eclipsed by that of his very remarkable sons.

Bruce designed a number of other country houses in the classic style; Harden in Teviotdale, Moncreiffe in Perthshire, Auchendinny in Midlothian are among the best known. This last was erected in 1707, Bruce's latest work. It is very small, and though a miniature of Hopetoun and Kinross—the oblong central block linked to side wings by curving walls—it is a remarkable return to the Scottish vernacular tradition, harled walls and slated roof, all ornament eschewed.

Of the persistence of the old ways about this time we have a most impressive example at Greenlaw, where in 1712 there was added to the church a vaulted tower to serve as prison, so much in the style of the late fifteenth century as to have deceived the very elect. It rises gaunt and unbuttressed, with a very prominent square stair-turret projecting from the centre of the east side. The parapet overhangs on a double row of corbels, actually with machicolations, most severe and plain. The door is square-headed and closed by a heavy iron grating, the bars all rectangular and riveted at each intersection. The hinges have massive wall staples, and there are two hasps, close together, one fixed, the other hinged. Above are four iron-bound windows, each lighting a different stage.

Meanwhile, in Edinburgh, Milne's Close in the Lawnmarket, dated 1690, had anticipated the lofty fronts of the eighteenth century. It is pierced by the plainest of windows, with monotony completely unrelieved, and as destitute of any enrichment as the most severe functional fabric of today.

William Adam was the most renowned of purely Scottish architects during the first half of the eighteenth century. The Old Town House, 'a Deidonanis extructa' in 1734, gave an atmosphere of the Scotland of a bygone day to the central section of Dundee till its most unfortunate destruction in 1931. On heavy round arches it spanned the side-walk. The central section slightly projected and had shallow Ionic pilasters, grouped in four pairs, carrying a pediment with the city arms. Behind rose a fine clock tower, square as it pierced the roof, with an octagonal spire above, the details very correct if a little undistinguished. The slated roof was not concealed and the large chimney-stacks were emphasised. The façade had channelled joints, but only in painted cement. The rest was good rubble. The rooms inside had rather undistinguished plasterwork in low relief.

This purely Scottish building was discarded in favour of exactly such a civic centre as may be seen in the larger prairie towns of the American West. No patriotic Scot can be expected to feel enthusiasm in seeing a famous old Scottish town desiring to range itself rather with Lincoln, Nebraska, or Des Moincs, Iowa, than with the ancient traditions of Caledonia. It leaves one of the oldest of

Scottish cities with hardly any other relics of its past than the splendid old church steeple and the Howff, as the walled burial place is called, on the site of the Franciscan friary. Some of its old monuments are almost as impressive and striking as those of the Edinburgh Greyfriars', but it would be unwise to say too much about them, seeing that in Scotland we have so many city fathers who seem to feel that if anything more than fifty years old is praised by antiquaries it ought probably in the interests of progress to be swept away at once. We know our local authorities!

The union of the two kingdoms under Anne made but little difference to the Scottish countryside, but Dr. Johnson's well-known jibe about the noblest prospect that a Scot ever sees being the high road that leads him into England was specially true of architects. Quite a number of the best-known English ones during the eighteenth century had passed along that way. It is a bit startling to come across, in an instrument of resignation among the title-deeds of Whim (under date February 12th, 1743), a reference to 'that part of his majesty's Kingdom of Great Brittain formerly called Scotland,' but such a formula does not seem to have been at all usual.

Although he was not greatly distinguished for his actual build-ings—and in his native Scotland he designed nothing of the slightest importance—no one did more for correct classic taste than Colin Campbell (d. 1729). He is chiefly remembered for his *Vitruvius Britannicus*, a book that did much for the study of the best traditions of the classic style. The mighty works of imperial Rome were, largely at any rate, the products of individual minds; the great building emperor, Hadrian, designed some of his fabrics himself. Unlike the Gothic of the Middle Ages, Rome's was not a communal art. It was thus exceedingly important that architects should have the opportunity of making themselves familiar with the details of the classic orders and with the rules that governed their use. Every-thing had to be rigid; the craftsman must do exactly as he was directed. The wide discretion allowed him in mediaeval building was perfectly out of the question. Thus the classic of the eighteenth century had a real life and inspiration that was impossible for the Gothic revival that followed. This could only have succeeded had

151 Grandtully Chapel, Perthshire

Mens pleasures fond, do promeis only Joyes;
Bor he that yeldes, at lengthe him selt destroyes.

152 Culross Palace, Fife

SCOTTISH PAINTED CEILINGS (EARLY SEVENTEENTH CENTURY)

153, 154 Fireplaces and Ceilings in Winton Castle, East Lothian

the craftsmen's tradition survived. The ancient spirit of Gothic was too elusive to be recaptured, and as the same sort of churches were still required there grew up a mere habit of copying. And it cannot be too strongly emphasised that, while the classic work was in direct historic continuity with the past, the Gothic revival was not.

James Gibbs (1682-1754) was born in Aberdeen and studied in Rome, whence he returned to take his place as the leading English architect of his day. One of his chief works is the Radcliffe camera at Oxford, a most admirable composition, while his church of St. Martin's-in-the-Fields (Trafalgar Square) is one of the very best of its kind, with its magnificent Corinthian portico and admirably managed internal decoration. His only important Scottish work, and his last, was the West Kirk on the site of the mediaeval nave of St. Nicholas', Aberdeen. It is a perfect example of correct classic in freestone, a little suggestive of copy-book design. The very plain ashlar façade, centre projecting and surmounted by a simple pediment, single portal beneath a large window, round-headed like all the rest, bold quoins with channelled joints, is a model of orthodox treatment. The nave of five bays, with aisles and leaded roofs above strong cornices, has a most satisfying effect. The interior recalls the best tradition of contemporary London churches, with Corinthian columns and architraves supporting barrel-vaulted centre and aisles with quadripartite bays. In place of the altar is a tall canopied throne for the lord provost, four Corinthian shafts supporting a pediment with the burgh arms. Though in a sense complete in itself, this fabric had to form the nave of a great cruciform mediaeval church, which has unfortunately been almost wholly (and very badly) rebuilt.

This is the best of the classic churches of Scotland. Such buildings are nearly negligible during the period with which this chapter is concerned. An admirable beginning of a distinctively Protestant architecture had been made at Burntisland as early as 1592 (during the first Presbyterian ascendency) obviously under Dutch inspiration, though it appears to be earlier than any similar fabric of Holland. An aisle extends the whole way round a central square, which could be carried up as a tower. Thus a convenient position for a pulpit is provided, but for an altar none. But the lead was not followed up; no other Scottish church on similar lines ever seems to have been erected. And unlike Protestant Holland, and even Puritan New England, Presbyterian Scotland evolved no religious art of any kind. The heritor system, which placed upon the landowners the obligation of housing the minister and his flock, tended less to architectural display than to the devising of means to fulfil the legal obligation at the lowest possible expense.

That is not to assert that no church erected during the period has any merit of design. At Durisdeer in Dumfriesshire there stands a most striking little building of rubble with ashlar quoins, having double transepts and a bold cornice. Over the centre of the western transept, intended for a school, there rises a square tower, and the effect is unusual and good. The date is given on a sundial, 1699. In the interior are the magnificent Queensberry monuments, including a marble baldachino with twisted columns by John Nost. At the model village of Gifford, erected when Yester was abandoned, there stands at the end of the broad village street a most picturesque T-shaped Dutch-looking church, built in 1710, the walls covered with white harling. The tower projecting from the middle of the long side, opposite the transept, has two stages, separated by a bold stringcourse and surmounted by an octagonal slated spire. It is unfortunate that this good vernacular building formed no tradition.

Almost the only individual feature of the village churches of the late seventeenth and eighteenth centuries in Scotland is the laird's loft, corresponding to the English parlour pew and such continental fabrics as the royal gallery in the cathedral at Turin. These might be decorated without offence. However superbly enshrined and lifted above the simple village folk, it was not seriously feared that they would mistake their laird for a saint. The fine panelling and other fittings from these lofts have usually been (sacrilegiously) appropriated to other uses in the church, but a few remain. At Bowden, under date 1661, we find a long and shallow gallery, supported on three posts and canopied by a rather eccentric pediment spread along the wall, with Ionic shafts, a cornice running across the gable. It would seem to the present generation to be difficult to sit there without self-consciousness. Indeed, it

rather suggests a child's rhyme which appeared many years ago
in the New York magazine called *St. Nicholas*:

> Hi! Pussies! Ho! Pussies! Are your faces clean?
> Don't you know you're sitting there
> So as to be seen?

The 'done thing' was for the laird to appropriate a chancel or
transept and there establish a gallery with the family vault beneath
it. A splendid example is to be seen at Abercorn, where the square-
ended Norman chancel is crossed by a beam with open fretwork
and festoons of flowers and fruit beneath; this opens to the large
capacious gallery of the Hopetoun family, whose arms are painted
on the ceiling with the motto 'AT SPES INFRACTA.' Adjoining is a
retiring-room panelled in Memel pine with Ionic pilasters and a
marble fireplace. A squint (or hagioscope?) which cuts into an
early chancel window allows a view of the pulpit so that the
minister's entry could be seen. This was designed by Bruce.

Sir William Chambers (1726-96), born in Stockholm, was of
Scottish descent, though chiefly resident in England and a member
of Johnson's circle. As a young man he visited China in a Swedish
vessel and became interested in the art of the East, afterwards
designing the well-known pagoda at Kew. He studied in Italy
and by his rebuilding of Somerset House gave London one of its
best classic monuments. He had less imagination than Gibbs; his
buildings rather lack originality. At Milton Abbey in Dorset he
made a disastrous effort at Gothic, incorporating the monastic
refectory, beside the ancient church. His only important Scottish
building is Duddingston House, now dedicated to golf. The actual
mansion is rather box-like and uninteresting, but it is redeemed by
a really admirable portico with four Corinthian columns and an
effective balustrade, obscuring the roofs behind; the details are
very good.

Longer than any other British town Edinburgh had remained
cramped and huddled within her walls. It is not easy to say just
why, for there was not even a tradition that they had ever kept an
enemy at bay. The fact had come out as clearly as well it could—
the castle could not be taken and the city could not be held. Bonnie
Prince Charlie in '45 revelled at Holyrood while the Georgian
army held the acropolis. And when the Hanoverian king again

possessed both, from their crowded quarters within the useless Flodden defences the citizens looked out across the open fields and asked themselves why they should not follow the lead of every other town.

Seven years after the Jacobite rising, in 1752, there was published a pamphlet: *Proposals for carrying on certain public works in the city of Edinburgh*. The title-page is anonymous, but the writer is known to have been Sir Gilbert Elliot, who bore the courtesy title of Lord Minto (1693-1766). He was a member of the 'committee of taste for the improvement of the town.' On page 7 it is complained that the Scottish capital 'Placed upon the ridge of a hill admits but of one good street, running from east to west, and even this is tolerably accessible only from one quarter. The narrow lanes leading to the north and the south, by reason of their steepness, narrowness and dirtiness, can only be considered as so many unavoidable nuisances. Confined by the small compass of the walls, and the narrow limits of the royalty, which scarcely extends beyond the walls, the houses stand more crowded than in any other town in Europe, and are built to a height that is almost incredible. Hence necessarily follows a great want of free air, light, cleanliness and every other comfortable accommodation. Hence also many families, sometimes no less than ten or a dozen, are obliged to live overhead of each other in the same building when to all the other inconveniences is added that of a common stair, it is no other in effect than an upright street, constantly dark and dirty.'

The romance of the site and the beauty of the surrounding hills are never hinted at; on the contrary, the utmost envy is expressed of the flat and unencumbered sites of the other two capitals, London and Dublin, which enable them to extend in suitable classic streets and squares. And this is no new discovery, for 'Mr. Fletcher of Salton, a very spirited and manly author, in his second discourse on the affairs of Scotland, written so long ago as the year 1698, has the same observation. "As the happy situation of London," says he, "has been the principal cause of the glory and riches of England; so the bad situation of Edinburgh has been one great occasion of the poverty and uncleanliness in which the greater part of the people of Scotland live."'

And so an assembly of magistrates, town council, college of

155 Airds, Argyll

156 Arniston, Midlothian

PALLADIAN INFLUENCE

157 Edinburgh University, Old Quadrangle. Started by Robert Adam
in 1789

justice, and other persons of rank 'came unanimously to be of opinion that a proper plan should immediately be drawn out of the improvements proposed to be made:

'1mo. To build upon the ruins on the north side of the high street an exchange with proper accommodation for our merchants.

'2do. To erect upon the ruins in the parliament close a large building containing such accommodations as are still wanting for the courts of justice, the royal boroughs [spelling *sic*] and town council, offices for the clerks, proper apartments for the several registers and for the advocates' library.

'3tio. To obtain an act of parliament for extending the royalty; to enlarge and beautify the town, by opening new streets to the north and south, removing the markets and shambles, and turning the North Loch into a canal with walks and terraces on each side.

'4to. That the expense of these public works should be defrayed by a national contribution.'

There were long delays, and it was not until 1767 that the competition for the best plan of laying out the new town was won by James Craig, a pupil of Sir Robert Taylor (founder of the Taylorian at Oxford), and his design duly published. Craig was a nephew of the poet, James Thomson, and he found his inspiration in some of his lines:

> August, around, what Public Works I see!
> Lo, stately streets! lo, squares that court the breeze!
> See long canals and deepened rivers join
> Each part with each, and with the circling main,
> The whole enlivened Isle.

The actual design is not inspired. The whole area between the Castle Rock and Queen Street is laid out in large rectangles with wide roads at right angles to each other. The Nor' Loch had already been drained (in 1763), but on its site was to be a broad and straight canal, the rectangles on either side being gardens. Farther north, George Street is intersected by Castle, Frederick, and Hanover Streets, which of course connect it with the splendid terrace which originally was to be called after St. Giles, but which George III suggested should be Princes Street, to give more aristocratic associations—as if the nomenclature were not already sufficiently Guelph. At the ends of George Street were to be the great squares that actually exist; these were to be called after St. Andrew and St. George, and the churches of those saints were to face each other, looking across the squares and down the street. St. George got his church, but lost the name of his square— supplanted by Queen Charlotte. St. Andrew kept his square, but his church was pushed out of it on to an inferior position on the north side of George Street. The actual site was occupied by Physicians' Hall, designed by Craig himself in 1775, but that in its turn has been ousted by the Royal Bank of Scotland.

Gardens were arranged beyond Queen Street and against the Calton Crag, and in this district the old Trinity Church was to be preserved. The Register House is shown facing the North Bridge, exactly where it is. A later development provided for a great circus in the middle of George Street, but this was never made. Every one was delighted with this splendid scheme, and a grateful royal burgh conferred upon Craig the freedom of the city with a gold medal. Sir Daniel Wilson in his *Memorials of Edinburgh* written a generation ago is very scornful and says the plan is commonplace, and not at all carefully aligned with the contours of the ground. This it is not very easy to deny. Roads extending straight up the slope from the Nor' Loch to Princes Street would have had impossible gradients, the formal parterres would have been abruptly cut off by the bottom of the Castle Rock. A more intensive survey of the site might easily have suggested improvements. To this generation, however, it can only be a matter for envy that the city fathers of that age wanted a plan at all and showed themselves so deeply concerned. We who have to see the city crawl unplanned and foul the finest near-by views with hideous bungaloids . . . And this is not the worst . . . !

It was certainly an advantage that the formal plan was not forced upon Princes Street Gardens, and still more that no effort was made to carry out a large-scale replanning of the old town. The Tron Kirk was designed to be the centre of a great octagon, which would have involved unfortunate destruction, while the great crescent beyond that was to have welcomed the traveller from the south and given an open site to the old quadrangle of the University might have had its advantages, but would have looked absurd when the city insisted upon creeping beyond it. And yet it is certainly unfortunate that George Square was allowed to stand alone, itself well planned, the surrounding streets almost entirely undesigned.

Whatever the faults of Craig's design, it did inspire further classic planning upon a noble scale from the Haymarket to Leith Walk and Calton Crag. It is, of course, a major disaster that the railways could not have been taken through the city well to the north or the south of the Castle Rock. Yet in the whole of the British Isles this great town planning of Edinburgh is rivalled at Bath alone, and even Ruskin, in his Edinburgh lectures (while missing lancet arches in the classic squares) could say: 'As far as I am acquainted with modern architecture I am aware of no streets which in simplicity and manliness of style or general breadth and brightness of effect, equal those of the New Town of Edinburgh.'

It seems that Craig himself designed the first parts of the new town to be built. They do not appear to have been monumental, and mostly they have been reconstructed. It was fortunate that abler designers were found to continue the work of making the new town a city that is at unity with itself. Most unhappily, it was not the fate of Princes Street to share the long continuous façades that exist in less conspicuous sections.

It was the very special merit of Robert Adam (1728-92) that he gave new forms to an architectural tradition that had become a little stale from having merely rehashed old designs since the death of the great Wren. He went to the fountain-head and, travelling in Dalmatia and Italy, became particularly interested in the vast palace of Diocletian at Spalatro (Split), the last great work of Rome before the Christian age, a fabric of the late third century of our era. Former students had concentrated more on the buildings of the earlier years between Augustus and Severus.

Robert Adam's foreign studies gave him a taste for rather intricate classic ornament, and especially all sorts of varieties of the Greek honeysuckle, executed in low relief. In collaboration with his less distinguished brothers he evolved what is largely a new classic school, rather eschewing porticoes and monotonous pilasters and substituting bold round arches (whether pierced or not), strong masses of plain masonry, making much of niches, floral festoons, lunettes, carefully designed cornices, and frequent roundels enclosing a conventionalised sunflower or framing a human head. Fireplaces were enriched with hanging garlands, oval ornaments, human figures breaking into foliaged forms, and many similar devices in very slight relief. Horace Walpole flippantly called them harlequinades. In his own Scotland Adam generally built in massive freestone and his designs are usually masculine and strong; when he went down into England, and was forced to use plaster and brick, a rather feminine elegance crept in. This is exactly characterised by Beresford Chancellor: 'The fact is that the Adam style is appropriate and, when not over-elaborated, charming for internal decoration, but lacks virility when applied to exteriors of large buildings.' * It would not be very easy exactly to illustrate this from any important Scottish structure, but it certainly is not wholly untrue of the very striking brick terraces and streets of the Adelphi district—almost the whole of which London has swept away to be replaced by importations from Chicago!

Perhaps the most pleasing feature of the new town at Edinburgh is Adam's monumental Charlotte Square, though its unity is rather lost by the very wide road openings at the four corners, which allow inferior lines of houses to obtrude into almost any view. The square is treated with single blocks on the north and the south, double ones on the other sides, occasioned by the openings occupied by the west end of George Street and by St. George's Church. All is ashlar, there is a rusticated basement, and above rise three storeys, the lower emphasised by channelled joints and the two upper having orders very sparingly employed. These take the form of pilasters at the ends and in the centre engaged columns, Ionic capitals west and east, and on the other sides a conventionalised hart's-tongue fern takes the place of the more hackneyed acanthus. The only pediments face each other north and south, resting upon the central four of groups of eight engaged columns. Bold round arches are introduced in various ways, but nearly all the windows are square-headed. Ornament is most sparingly and carefully introduced, such as bulls' heads with garlands and roundels enclosing human forms; on the north two sphinxes give a sort of added repose to the parapet. There is a restraint and good taste

* *Lives of British Architects*, p. 306.

about the whole which makes the effect exceedingly satisfactory. Unfortunately St. George's Church (by Robert Reid), erected 1811-1814, which ought to be the climax of the whole design, comes a little short. Between two blocks of masonry is a fairly well-managed Ionic colonnade, but above rises a rather thin columned drum with dome above which merely surmounts the vestibule quite uselessly. The actual church has a much lower dome which does not show outside.

One of the best of Robert Adam's works is the old quadrangle of Edinburgh University, dated 1789. The strong ashlar façade has basement with channelled joints and two storeys with emphasised cornices and several pedimented windows. The massive central block is pierced by a triple vaulted gate, flanked by stone galleries on columns, a great lunette above. The lofty dome that surmounts it was only finished some fifty years ago, under the direction of Rowand Anderson. The design was largely modified by W. H. Playfair (1789-1857), who carried on Adam's work here as elsewhere. He is a most interesting figure as among the last great architects of the classic era and also one of the early revivers of Gothic. As finished by him, the interior presents a single oblong court, four separate blocks connected by corner curves, arched cloisters below and open colonnades above. The place of the basement is taken by a surrounding terrace with appropriate flights of steps, and there are shallow porticoes in the centres of the two long sides. The building would have a most monumental effect if seen across a country park, down a long avenue of trees. But it stands among crowded city streets; it is dug into the hillside very awkwardly; and it can only be inspected at the risk of being hit by a passing motor.

The Register House, another work of Robert Adam, is rather less happy in its design, while far more fortunate in its site. It has the interesting feature of reviving the Scottish tradition of slightly projecting towers at the angles and in the centre of each side, as at Heriot's Hospital. But in the façade a pedimented block with Corinthian pilasters takes the place of a tower, and there is a similar arrangement at the back. There are two storeys over a basement, and the work is severe and plain. Turrets rise over the corner towers, those in the front displaying wind-dial and clock.

There is little doubt that the Lord Chief Baron of the Scottish Exchequer, Sir James Montgomery (1721-1803), employed Adam for his works at Whim in Peeblesshire, though unfortunately the title-page is missing from the contemporary book of alternative plans. The mansion, oblong in plan and rising three storeys above the basement plinth, heavily corniced and displaying huge chimney-stacks rising through the flat roof centre, bears a striking resemblance to Melville House, Ladybank, Fife, the joint work of Bruce and a far less known man named James Smith. The effect is, however, inferior from the Peeblesshire house having smooth cement or ashlar instead of the traditional harling. The façade of whim square is nevertheless one of the best works of its time; the long, plain, ashlar front relieved by bold niches and presenting pediments with pilasters at the ends, in the centre a gateway ingeniously piercing a portico whose pediment rests upon two pairs of widely detached columns admirably proportioned and with capitals of hart's-tongue leaves. The projected central clock tower was never built. The great neighbouring mansion of Penicuik, which has one of the finest porticoes in all Scotland, was erected by Sir James Clerk about 1770. He employed Alexander Runciman to paint the ceilings with the Ossian legends and scenes from the life of St. Margaret. This work is said to have been very fine, but it perished in the fire of forty years ago,* since which the house has been a ruined shell. The contemporary square, over whose gateway rises a classic steeple refused for the parish church, has been turned into a delightful residence enclosing an Italian garden. Sir James was a keen antiquary, and the replica of Arthur's O'on which forms the centre of one of the sides gives the fabric an exceedingly original effect.

In 1819 Playfair published his report on the further laying out of the New Town. It deals with the district beside Calton Crag. It led to the planting of gardens on the steeper slopes and to his designing the really most effective façades of Royal and Regent Terraces. Left to himself, he preferred the old classic use of pilasters and engaged columns to the tradition that the Adams had

---

* It must be confessed that Runciman's existing wall paintings in the eastern apse of the Edinburgh church now known as St. Patrick's do not give a very favourable impression of his work. But they were subsidiary to others in the dome, which is now destroyed.

left. It was undoubtedly far easier. He was also employed to design the Royal Scottish Academy and the National Gallery on the Mound. Both are good classic work without any great distinction. The former has Doric colonnades, for the rather short-lived vogue for Greek rather than Latin forms was not fully established. Ruskin strongly criticised its very inconspicuous conventional lions' heads along the frieze, but it is very doubtful whether the absolutely natural ones which he advocated with so much vehemence and satire would have given a more satisfactory effect. The National Gallery, behind the other, is much more Roman in design, with rather ordinary Ionic porticoes. In the academy at Dollar (1818), superbly placed under the towering mass of the Ochils, Playfair produced another classic design of singular dignity. The chief façade centres in a fine hexastyle portico with Tuscan columns, and this gives access to a vestibule that is ingeniously modelled on the Pantheon at Rome.

The late eighteenth century saw a number of minor works in the fading classic style, but they are of no outstanding interest or charm. St. Andrew's at Glasgow, by Mungo Naesmith, is a rough copy of St. Martin's-in-the-Fields, especially in the placing of a fragment of an entablature over each column of the interior and in the management of the roof above, but it is very inferior to the original. The exterior order is composite with a hexastyle portico, and a rather feeble classic steeple rises almost timidly above.

By this time Scotland had become the home of a more remarkable literary movement than moved the London of that day—when Johnson's goodly company were passing from the stage. It was centred very largely in Edinburgh; it is connected chiefly with the immortal name of Scott, and it was inspired in no small degree by that almost leafless grey old town with its time-worn mediaeval atmosphere of Gothic gables and lofty rubble walls, where, more almost than in any other place on earth, dour buildings are matched with rugged nature. In striking contrast, across the old Nor' Loch another sister town had risen in classic pomp, gardened beyond all others in the west, built as a town that shares one grand design.

Edinburgh was a chief centre of the romantic revival. This was a reaction against a classicism from which real life had very largely ebbed, and a new enthusiasm for everything mediaeval. Its earliest prophet is generally said to have been the poet Gray, just as Roger Bacon and Dante, who both passed their lives amid purely mediaeval surroundings, were in different ways pioneers of the Renaissance. But so far as this country is concerned, the chief inspiration of the movement was in the writings of Sir Walter Scott and others, while the religious movement that was inaugurated at Oxford in 1833 was at least in the same direction.

A craze for the revival of Gothic architecture now set in, which has few defenders today. For it gave us nothing but transparent sham, not even at Abbotsford itself. The classic tradition was the last of the living styles because it came down in never entirely broken tradition from the very earliest times; it was the archi-tecture, while it lasted, of well-nigh the whole nation. The build-ings of the Gothic revival were chiefly sponsored by individual caprice; their monuments are apt to be dead and uninteresting, quite out of keeping with what has gone before. The new builders could see little difference between the real and the sham, and were quite content to copy stone vaulting in plastered lathing. They frequently saw no objection to the substitution of modern copies for mediaeval work itself.

It is remarkable that in Scotland the same architect, Playfair, was both among the last of the classicists and the first of the votaries of neo-Gothic. Following the fashions of the Tudors, he built New College above his galleries on the Mound, and in imitation of Heriot's he built Donaldson's Hospital.

Gillespie Graham (c. 1777-1855) was also prominent in intro-ducing the new style. It appears to have been with the help of Pugin that he designed the Tolbooth Church (Assembly Hall) at Edinburgh with its tolerable copy of the steeple of St. Mary Red-cliffe at Bristol, though the work has been claimed for Thomas Hamilton (1785-1858), who built the classic High School. Graham certainly designed the Roman Catholic cathedral at Glasgow with its impressive plaster-vaulted interior. Archibald Elliot built St. Paul's, York Place, in very feeble imitation of King's College Chapel at Cambridge, and William Burn (1789-1870) made an appalling mess of restoring St. Giles', destroying almost every original feature on the exterior. He did better with St. John's, Princes Street, whose interior is queerly effective. By the time

158 Charlotte Square (end of eighteenth century). Built from designs by Robert Adam

159 Moray Place: the dignity of the early nineteenth century

EDINBURGH, THE NEW TOWN

160 George Street

161 Law Courts (early nineteenth century)

CLASSICAL EDINBURGH

162 Regent Arch, Edinburgh.   A fine classical arch of the early
nineteenth century

163 Dollar Academy, Clackmannanshire. Built by W. H. Playfair in 1818

164 Calton Hill, Edinburgh. Left: the National Monument (1822)
Right: the Nelson Tower (1815)

Sir Gilbert Scott built St. Mary's Cathedral, also at Edinburgh, men had learned far more exactly to copy mediaeval work. The rectangular quire has the distinction of being vaulted apsidally, for which a thirteenth-century precedent may be found in the crypt chapel at the Houses of Parliament. All these buildings follow purely English models, but Macgregor Chalmers at least had the merit of trying to work on lines familiar to Scotland, seeking to develop the traditions of Celtic Romanesque.

The first architect really to make a serious attempt at developing the mediaeval work of Scotland was, however, Sir Robert Lorimer, a pupil of Rowand Anderson. Almost perhaps for the first time, the special forms of the peculiarly Scottish form of Gothic are made to live again in the apsidal shrine of the War Memorial on Edinburgh Castle Rock. And that building is generally held to be one of the fairest of all the monuments that commemorate the World War.

The story of Scotland for more than a thousand years is written in her time-worn stones—for timber and brick she had but little use. Much stands today, and yet her monuments have suffered worse than those of almost every other land. Most of her noblest churches lie gaping to the skies.

But enough remains to prove that her building tradition was very much her own. And this account will not have been in vain if it helps to preserve what yet survives for generations yet to be.

INDEX

The numerals in *italics* denote the figure numbers of the illustrations